unstoppable
joy

unstoppable
JOY

The Art of Finding Hope, Healing, and Happiness

Dr. Nicole M. Robinson

Foreword By: Natasha L. Frye

purposely created PUBLISHING

Special discounts are available on bulk quantity purchases by book clubs, associations and special interest groups. For details email: sales@publishyourgift.com or call (888) 949-6228.

For information log on to:
www.PublishYourGift.com

To my almighty Lord, my wonderful mother, Sandra Land,
and my beloved grandparents, Cleophas and Leila Land.
To my loving family, my soulmate Aaron Ferguson,
and all individuals struggling with their mental health.
I love you all.

Table of Contents

Foreword

By Natasha L. Frye

Everyone has friends that come and go. When things get rough, people—those so-called friends—tend to stray. There are people that will judge you. There are people that will make you feel bad for expressing yourself. Yet there's always that one person with whom you happen to cross paths, who changes your life forever.

I believe God has a funny way of bringing people together. I bonded with my sister and best friend today through an unexpected encounter. I live in a house in northern Virginia, where roommates move in and out constantly. I had no idea that one roommate who moved in as a doctoral student would make such a huge impact.

At first, we didn't really say much. Gradually, we found ourselves confiding in each other with conversations that lasted for hours. Then one day I was told she was moving back home to Buffalo, New York. We hung out and chatted as much as we could until it was time for us to say goodbye.

It's funny how a friendship can flourish when everyone is gone and all is silent.

When she left, it seemed as if our friendship grew stronger.

During the good times, we were there for each other. When she received her doctorate in 2012, I was there to cheer her on as she walked across the stage. I was so proud of a young woman not even 30 years old making such a great mark in her life … and the world. When my own family was not there to cheer me on as I received my master's degree, she was there for support.

In bad times, we saw each other through the pain.

On September 12, 2014, I was at my lowest. I was hit by a drunk driver. Upon graduating, I had received no job offers. I had no money, no food, and no car. My body went numb, and I didn't want to deal with life anymore. Then, everything went dark.

I had a box cutter, and I started to cut myself.

I reached out to many people, but she was the only one who answered. She stayed on the phone with me for hours trying to get me to a hospital. I refused, but she never gave up on me. Upon hanging up, she contacted crisis services in my area. As a result, two police officers showed up at my door to help me.

She was in another state, but she saved my life.

Did I want to die?

No.

I merely wanted someone to show she cared.

Even after the incident, my friend never judged or asked questions; she simply accepted me.

Although we've gone through many hardships over the years, we've always managed to keep each other encouraged. I've never met someone so full of compassion, and her caring nature extends well beyond our friendship into the classroom. As one of the most humble and intelligent minds I've ever encountered, she is among the greatest professors any student could ask for in higher education.

Her name is Nicole Robinson, Ph.D., or as I call her, "the good doctor."

I'm so honored to call her my friend, my sister, my angel.

Reflections of Imperfection

Never good enough, never to be

The person in the mirror is not she

The woman who was is clearly long gone

a different being now belongs.

Behind all the laughter refreshed anew,

the smiles she hopes you'll continuously view,

Lies darkness down in the center of mind

that holds a pain scale marked one–of–a–kind.

Beyond love and care found deep in her heart,

many often miss the most ironic part.

The love she feels for everyone else

is the very same love she can't give to herself.

They say she's a blessing—tender loving and dear.

She can't recognize qualities she refuses to hear.

They don't seem to fit the mirror's reflection.

It screams unworthiness; no love, no affection.

Until she believes, she'll fight off the sorrow,

holding hands with her Lord to face another tomorrow.

If those she loves can love her in distress,

then she can keep hope for true happiness.

Introduction

"The toughest lesson in finding joy is learning how to let go of the desire to lead a perfect life in an imperfect world. True happiness evolves when you allow yourself to see the beauty in those imperfections."

For over 20 years, I've dealt with depression.

I'm not talking about the "I have a pimple, so I refuse to go out the house today" type of depression. I'm talking about the type of sadness that asks, "What's the point of leaving the house at all?"

For the longest time, I thought of joy like perfection—you try your best to obtain it, but everyone knows you can never reach it. Thus, I managed my depression like many people within the African American community. I labeled it "stress," brushed it off, and kept moving. I wasn't content with my life, but I desperately tried to make the necessary adjustments.

Until one day I grew tired of being sad.

I was sick and tired of being sick and tired.

At some point, it actually became easier for me to tackle the reason I was unhappy instead of staying that way. Finally, I was ready to be honest with myself. Glancing in the mirror, I murmured the words my soul had been longing to hear: "I'm the hold up. I'm the only person stopping myself from being happy."

Needless to say, admitting the harsh truth that I didn't want to be happy was a life-changing experience. There was a sense of comfort in neglecting happiness. Actually, I had been taught to ignore my mental health since childhood. I thought being unhappy made me stronger. If I never accepted joy, then I was already prepared for the tough times. If I hung on to disappointment, then I could face the difficulties of life with ease. If that was the case, then I didn't want to take a chance on being happy only to lose it dealing with life's obstacles. Why even try?

That's when I learned that the toughest lesson in finding joy is learning how to let go of the desire to lead a perfect life in an imperfect world. I became fully aware that true happiness evolves when you allow yourself to see the beauty in those imperfections. I had to be open to experiencing joy in spite of my situation. I became aware that joy was never based on my circumstances, but, instead, on my willingness to accept it. It was a decision I had to make on a daily basis.

Instead of choosing joy, I decided that having depression meant living in misery. I was waiting for the depression to go away before I began the work of feeling better. Essentially, I settled for defeat. I made depression part of my personality, and my attitude toward life followed right along. Feeling depressed was just another emotion, and unfortunately, it was the dominant one. All the while, I didn't realize I had the power to fight that mentality. Mental distress didn't have to steal my joy. I made the choice that it would not win. It would no longer hold power over me.

You see, joy is a state of mind. How you get to experience that state requires you to do some soul searching. Whether you are just feeling lost or suffering from depression, it's still a mindset. You just need to find what puts you in the right frame of mind to receive the joy you crave. It may be harder to do in some cases, but you can still live a life of victory. As for me, I had to visualize my picture of joy, and then start making moves toward living it.

Today, many question how I could manage the challenges I faced. They wonder how I could hold so many accomplishments yet still have the time to help others dealing with the same mental distress—often talking people out of potential meltdowns, utter despair, and even suicide.

While I'm not a therapist, I believe my gift of encouragement provides the inspiration others need when they are ready to throw in the towel.

It has always been my desire to share that gift.

The result is a book filled with years of experience that will help people of all walks of life find joy. I'm not talking about life coaching based off a few months of hopelessness or a month of despair. I'm talking about advice from an author who doesn't have to be told to walk in someone else's shoes because she has a pair of her own. I mean encouragement from someone who can hit rock bottom and still climb to the top—someone who can experience joy while battling an ache that threatens to steal that happiness every day.

The trick is to know that for every problem there is a key to a door that opens a room full of solutions. We just have to figure out which key opens the door we need. Depression, low self-esteem, emptiness, mood swings, loss of purpose, discouragement, or even anxiety comes with a solution that works. Your job is to find the solution that works best for you given your personality, experiences, thought patterns, and basic understanding of how this "finding happiness" thing works.

You will see that this book is designed to meet you where you are in your journey. You don't have to struggle with depression to enjoy this book. You may be struggling to find the meaning of your life or your purpose. You may desire a boost in self-esteem. You may benefit from the encouragement offered on forgiveness and dealing with negative situations. Perhaps you simply have a desire to lead a more fulfilling life (or want to help someone else do the same). Whatever the case, this book is for you.

I don't believe you stumbled upon this book by accident. You were drawn to it for a reason. There is something in this book that is meant to change your life for the better, since it has definitely changed mine.

So, let's get started on your journey to joy.

You are well worth the trip.

Chapter One:

Preparing for the Journey

> "Everyone has unique circumstances and trials, but with them come the unique talents and characteristics to deal with them."

Imagine you at your very best. Joy is no longer in the distance, but close enough for you to grab.

What would it take to get there? What would you need for the journey?

One thing is for sure: you would have to be full of hope to embark on that adventure. You would need to be secure in knowing you exist for a greater purpose. You would have the ability to let go of unrealistic expectations from people and things to make you happy. Instead, you would be able to find happiness on your own terms. You would definitely have a clear picture of what joy meant to you, and you would strive each day to live out that vision.

Along your journey, you would find that in spite of your circumstances, you would need to maintain an optimistic attitude about the future. As a matter of fact, you'd be so excited about what's to come that you would prepare for those joyous occasions before they arrived. Even if you ran into some difficult, painful moments while getting there, you wouldn't let them keep you down. You would learn from them and get back up.

You would understand that joy equals power, and you would be determined not to give that power away to anyone or anything. You would be an expert in managing your emotions, with the ability to tune out the negativity that can disrupt your peace of mind. You would have a sense of confidence as you stop comparing yourself to others and slowly let go of past hurts. At last, you would see your full worth ... your full potential. This would cause you to value yourself enough to take care of your most pressing needs by having a plan in place to rejuvenate so you can fully enjoy all that life has to offer.

That's how you live a life that spells out true happiness:

H ope in a Consistent Source of Power

A ccept Reality versus Expectations

P repare for Emotional Roadblocks

P aint Your Own Picture of Joy

I dentify Yourself as Valuable

N o to Negative Thinking

E at Well, Plan Well

S elf-Care is a Must

S ecure a Safety Plan

I believe that you don't have to imagine anymore. You can live your best life now. It is there for the taking. It may seem like you can't get through another sleepless night. It may seem like you can't forgive that person. It may seem like you can't learn to love yourself. However, I'm here to tell you that it can be done. Everyone has unique circumstances and trials, but with them come the unique talents and characteristics to deal with them. You are much stronger than you think. You are not only worthy of happiness, but you deserve to be happy. I'm determined to show you how to claim that happiness.

Chapter Two:

Hope in a Consistent Source of Power

> *"When we make other people or things our only source of power, they don't help us. They control us."*

Hold on tight! Similar to strapping yourself in before a roller coaster ride, you should also make sure to do the same before tackling life's issues and goals. I would be lying if I said that happiness lies only with you, because it doesn't work that way. As humans, we need a power that is greater than our own. If we could handle life alone, then we would be the only human on the planet. We would do everything by ourselves in the best mood at all times.

In reality, we are limited. We may have some control over how we choose to respond and what we expose ourselves to daily, but full control is impossible. Humans are wired that way, and that's okay. The important step is to realize we need this inner power or we will be constantly fighting unnecessary battles. When we exhaust ourselves doing so, we take away the strength or ability to tackle the problems that we can handle.

If you want to know how to push through when times get rough, you must accept that you can't do this on your own. There will be times that seem hopeless. There will come a time when you see no possible way out. There will come a time when you are giving one hundred percent and it's still not enough. You will find yourself sitting there with nowhere to turn. That is when the acknowledgement or hope in something or someone stronger than you comes into play.

The 12-step program used by many addiction support groups emphasizes this important point in living a well-balanced life; the first step states that you must consider a power greater than yourself. You must accept that your willpower is not enough to beat your addiction. Why would this be the first step? Why couldn't they just list a higher power as the tenth step instead?

Simply, acknowledgement in a higher power is a constant reminder that we can't make it on our own strength. Taking on all the other steps toward fulfillment requires power outside of us. We can't get past the first step until we understand that it takes something bigger to make it through the remaining steps.

Thus, the first thing that needs to happen to gain strength is to lose some control. We need to let go of the notion that we can handle everything on our own power. We need to submit that control to a higher power that can guide us when we start to feel all is lost. Realizing that there is a greater force at work when we fall short makes all the difference.

This book is meant to be for those from all backgrounds, but I will share that my personal faith in the Lord has come to my rescue many times. I know it may sound cliché, but you are going to have to find the higher power that helps you when you can't help yourself. It can be God, Jesus Christ, a general knowledge of a higher power or a power greater than yourself, the universe, destiny, or your guardian angel. You can rely on whatever power you are comfortable relying on.

The only requirement is that your power source remains "on" or consistent at all times. Think of it as a light to help you see your way to joy and peace. When other lights turn off, the higher power in which you believe becomes the backup generator that permits you to continue when you feel there are no options left. It is your fuel.

The tips in this book are helpful, but I would not have accomplished so much in the past two decades with depression by relying on my own strength. For me, it's just not possible. Many others will tell you the same thing about their experiences. I'm convinced that social support is important for battling mental distress and maintaining good emotional health. However, I am also convinced that outside power is needed when that social support system can't fulfill every need.

Say you are up at 2:00 a.m. You may have friends who tell you it is okay to call anytime, but it's often hard to do that when you already feel like a burden. What if you are going through a problem that you don't feel comfortable telling anyone about? What if you want to talk and all of your friends are busy?

I state that this power should be constant because if we put our hope and strength into inconsistency, then we are setting ourselves up for extreme disappointment. Consequently, when we make other people or things our only source of power, they don't help us; they control us. It's like giving someone the keys to your car. They decide where you go, when you leave, and how long it's going to take to arrive. As they take our happiness and do whatever they want with it, we actually lose power. If they leave, our happiness goes with them.

It's so easy to do, but we have to be careful about whether that source is going to be there for us 24/7/365. That means that this higher power cannot be our parents, spouse/significant other, children, friends, etc. That means that it is not found in cosmetics, clothes, cars, money, technology, food, or alcohol. All of these sources are temporary. There's no long-lasting feeling of fulfillment. Our parents aren't there all the time, and our significant other can't be emotionally supportive every day. You will also rack up a ton of debt chasing after things that make you feel good now in exchange for misery later.

Those who experience joy know not to put their hope into things that come and go. They know that if they do, that hope will be tossed about in every direction. That is because while you think these things help, they actually weigh you down as you try to hold on to them. Similar to the roller coaster example, you can't ask your friend two cars behind you to hold your hand when riding along, but you will grip the handle bars because they are something you can count on to always be there. You will hang on even when it's just you and those handlebars, waiting for the ride to slow down.

You get through because you aren't looking every which

way to calm your nerves. You simply stay strapped in and know that no matter what you can always grab the handle-bar in front of you. You can stop using your energy to find anyone and anything to assist you. You can focus on using that thing in front of you that constantly keeps you locked in. That's what a constant belief source does: it keeps you locked in to hope even when there appears to be none in sight.

You see, we are so quick to throw in the towel when the pain hits or when the uncertainty creeps in, because we look to ourselves to fix the situation. This causes us to feel powerless and leads to feelings of helplessness or hopelessness (which are some symptoms of depression). You get this feeling of emptiness that you can't seem to fill. Our first response is, "I can't do this anymore," or "I don't see a way out." However, sometimes, it's not up to us to fix the situation or find a way out at that exact moment. Quite possibly, it may take more than just the little strength that we have to keep fighting.

We are humans, not the energizer bunny.

When moments of despair creep up on us, we need to trust that higher power to complete what we can't do. We need to let God handle our problems. We need to let destiny or the universe work things out. Therefore, we need to see those opportunities not as a reason to quit, but as a chance to recharge so we can keep fighting.

WHAT'S THE POINT OF EXISTING?

"Asking yourself if this is all there is to your life is the equivalent of asking a realtor if the hallway you are standing in is all there is to see in a house."

~~~~~~~

A lack of hope often leads us to believe there's no point to life. We ask questions like, "Why do I even exist?" This is why I believe there's a need for a source outside of our own power—some of the deepest, most pressing questions we pose can't be answered on our own limited knowledge of how life works. Self-reflection is good, but we only hold a piece of the puzzle.

Don't confuse right now with why you are on this earth entirely. Your reason for existing isn't a straightforward answer. It's usually a collection of experiences, people, and events that determine why you are needed. Some of those experiences you haven't even discovered yet. Some of those people you haven't met yet. Some events aren't prepared for you at this time, but that doesn't mean they aren't scheduled to occur.

Let me put it this way: it's like walking into a house and deciding not to move in based on what you see from the front door. Suddenly, you make the decision you shouldn't be there based on what you see from where you are standing rather than taking a tour of the house.

You can't say, "Oh, this house isn't for me. Nice hallway though."

Similarly, you can't say, "Oh, this life isn't cut out for me."

Deep down, you know that the miracle of you being here was no coincidence. So, asking yourself if this is all there is to your life is the equivalent of asking a realtor if the hallway is all there is to see in a house. You usually make the decision to walk around before forming an opinion. You make a decision to buy the home based on many factors.

You are here for a reason, but you have to go through experiences or take a tour of your life to know that. I know some of you are thinking that you've been on a tour of your life and find there are many factors leading to nowhere. That's not true. You are touring each day. You are learning and experiencing things with every moment. If you've ever purchased a home, you know that you are still discovering things about your house years after you buy it. You are aware of the ability to transform or remodel. You also understand how the neighborhood or the environment can change at any moment.

Life works in the same way.

So, why are you basing your existence on where you are standing right now?

I would have highly disagreed with you at the age of 25 if you told me there was more to life. Then I moved out-of-state, received a doctorate, joined a sorority, and met my best friend. All of this happened when I was certain that everything I would experience in life had already occurred. I was obviously wrong.

Therefore, your existence isn't based off pure emotion. It isn't based off what you feel or believe at the time. There are people who need you now. There are people who are going to need you in the future. You exist for many reasons, and those reasons will be revealed to you at the appropriate time. However, if you aren't here, then you will never know those reasons.

Trust me, they are waiting to be revealed.

WHAT'S MY PURPOSE?

"Your being uncertain at the moment doesn't mean your purpose is uncertain."

~~~~~~~

As we seek our purpose in life, a loss of hope can often lead to major frustration. We often ask why we exist, but we also ask what we should do while we are here. I've learned that finding your purpose isn't necessarily the frustrating part; it's the waiting. It's really the time between picking up clues to your purpose and actually seeing those ideas become a reality. The in-between time is when we start to second-guess ourselves. It's when we start to doubt our ability. It's when we refuse to believe the advice of others when they tell us that things will get better. It's when we question our talents or struggle with our faith.

All of that is normal.

Therefore, we don't struggle with our sense of purpose.

We struggle with the unknown. Uncertainty scares us. It's the reason why people who fear the future develop anxiety. It's the reason why those who dwell on the past become depressed. You don't know the future. You don't know how your past will affect that future. You also don't know if what's ahead will be better than the present moment. As long as you can't see it, it remains unknown. However, your being uncertain at the moment doesn't mean your purpose is uncertain. Your purpose is rather secure.

Just like questioning the point of life, your purpose is also not so straightforward. It unfolds over a period of years or decades. In fact, you may have multiple purposes depending on when you decide to question it. That is because when you question your purpose you are really asking:

What should I do during this time?

What's my significance to those I meet?

What's my contribution to the world?

That's really not a one-time deal, and your purpose doesn't just involve you at any given moment. Think of the house example we used for exploring our existence. Imagine that the purpose of that house is for a family to create memories every Christmas. Someone in that family could take those experiences to establish a career that could help someone else. It may even cause the family to adopt a child who otherwise would not have a home.

Yet the architect doesn't know that he's part of that purpose when he's designing the house. The contractor doesn't know that when he's pouring concrete to construct the basement. The interior designer doesn't know when picking out the color of the dining room walls. The realtor may have some idea when handing over the keys, but really he or she wouldn't know until that family settled in.

A collection of rather small events that we would deem unimportant creates a domino effect. Thus, your purpose is performed in simple acts that often go unnoticed but have the potential to change the lives of those around you. It's a chain of events that add up to more than we can imagine. The full extent of your impact is not just the effects of what you see or the things within your reach. Your purpose is not solely based on your job title, relationship status, bank account, material possessions, or random achievements. Your purpose is summed up in this mystery: You never know whom you are influencing, what kind of impression you make, and how you can change a life without any intention of doing so.

That's why we become frustrated when we try to narrow down our purpose to one event or underestimate the roles we play. By narrowing down, I mean we base our purpose on one long-lasting, specific event, talent, or personality trait. We want a purpose that makes us popular or famous. We want a purpose that will show up in our bank account or appear while we are in front of a sold-out crowd. While that is the purpose for some, it is not the purpose for all.

I hear so many people say they don't make a difference because they are just a mother or just a small business owner trying to pay the bills. They think it doesn't matter that they are just cashiers. However, within those roles is the powerful ability to change lives. For instance, being a parent requires someone to raise a child to be a respectable, loving human being. Being a cashier allows you to affect every person who comes in to buy groceries.

About four years ago, I had a conversation with a shuttle driver. His job was to take customers home while their car was being serviced at the dealership and then pick them up when their car was ready. However, he wasn't just a driver to me. He touched my life. He told me a powerful story about his wife recovering from cancer by choosing to eat a raw diet. That story gave me hope. It made me question the foods I consumed. Gradually, I started switching to organic, all-natural products. Without even knowing it, he persuaded me to live a healthier lifestyle.

You might also recall the news story of a bus driver in my hometown of Buffalo, New York, who stopped a woman from committing suicide. She was standing on a bridge overlooking the expressway that just happened to be along his route that day. He was able to stop the bus and talk the woman off the ledge. He may have gone to work that day with the intention of getting people from point A to point B. However, on that day, his purpose was to stop someone from ending her life.

Now that's what you call a pretty big purpose.

I don't believe people are placed on this planet with no purpose whatsoever. I think people are just so busy trying to find their purpose that they don't see the little things they do that make a huge impact. Much like finding joy, we don't sit around and wait for our purpose to happen. We live it. We stop waiting for people to tell us our purpose in life. We stop trying to decide what encounters will have an impact. We simply live out our story with each day that passes. Every day, we are changing lives without even knowing it. Therefore, we don't need the recognition or the confirmation to know we have a specific purpose. All we really need is the assurance that we are living it out with each breath.

Chapter Three

Accept Reality over Expectations

> "We give life a ransom note with our list of demands,
> and refuse to cooperate if those demands aren't met."

Facing reality seems like it will decrease your happiness, but it actually boosts your mental health. The more you accept reality, the better you are at dealing with life's obstacles. One of my close friends was always chipper no matter what was going on in her life. I asked her how she did it, to which she responded, "I don't expect anything from anyone, so there are never any disappointments. If they actually do something, then that's great too."

I've started approaching life in the same manner. I believe we experience disappointment after disappointment when we hold unrealistic expectations over others or anticipate certain events. Most of us do this without even telling the person what we expect of them. We expect our partner to read between the lines or read our minds. Life just doesn't work that way. Life isn't a Disney fairytale (and, as a woman, I am guilty of believing that it was at one point in time). I'm sure Cinderella's happily ever after was also full of days where she was upset at Prince Charming for not being charming enough when he forgot their anniversary. He was probably even more upset that her stepsisters made a habit of stopping by unannounced.

We think things are perfect, but we can't expect perfection all the time.

The point is that our lives are nothing but a series of potential expectations with reality as the backdrop. When our expectations and reality don't align, we get upset. It would be okay in some cases if our reality didn't align with our expectations. However, in the real world, they won't perfectly align at every moment. We have to be flexible. Just like we wanted to be Batman or an X-Men character when we were children, we learned how to adjust those goals based on our given realities. We learned that there were no superheroes, so maybe we decided that being a firefighter was more realistic. That's why we don't see 35-year-olds walking around in bat suits. At some point in our growth, we find a way to accept and come to terms with our realities.

Yet there are many instances in which it's harder to come to terms with that reality. We may not walk around wearing a cape, but we tend to get sucked into this unrealistic expectation society has when it comes to certain wants from people and things. It's like we give life a ransom note with our list of demands and refuse to cooperate if those demands aren't met. We insist that it happen. In fact, we insist that it happen the way we would like and at the precise time we think it should occur. Then reality steps in and ruins everything.

In today's society, we have learned to expect that people and material things will make us happy. We've seen in many cases that codependency or counting on your partner to meet all your needs and wants is very unhealthy. It can lead to a stressful relationship or marriage, as your partner has the impossible job of making you happy all the time. Yet many of us get into relationships expecting that to happen. Either that or we find ourselves buying that new coat we think will make us look awesome. Then, a few weeks later, we feel like we don't have everything we need to really look awesome because the excitement from our purchase has worn off. It's a game that never ends.

I teach media courses, and I often ask my students to point out times when the media created or increased our expectations. The lesson usually ends up pointing out various traditions that in isolation are fine, but are presented in a way that makes us feel we need to do or have something to be happy. For example, Black Friday has made it so that you can eat and give thanks for what you have and then head to the mall to buy more items. We do it because of the sales. We rationalize our behavior by telling ourselves we need gifts for the upcoming Christmas holiday. Yet, aside from arguing with the person in line over a 42" television, we've made it so we aren't comfortable sitting with the things we claim to be thankful for long enough before the urge to accumulate more begins. You have a roof over your head and a dinner table full of food, but that television is in heavy demand by midnight. Seriously, on Thanksgiving night, I saw someone steal a man's television while his back was turned because it was the last one in stock.

My students also thought of Valentine's Day. Many of my male students complained that they dreaded all the commercials because it meant they were in trouble if they didn't get their partners the best gifts. They were in constant competition to live up to societal standards of what it meant to be a good partner. It's pretty awkward when you are sitting next to your girlfriend and a jewelry commercial comes on urging you to propose with a diamond ring (particularly one from a collection you can't afford). Now you almost feel obligated if that's what you feel is expected of you. And your girlfriend is instantly upset when she only gets candy and roses.

We also noticed another important point about Valentine's Day. If it weren't for the media and other people celebrating the holiday, we wouldn't know that February 14th was the official day to show our loved ones we care. Now we upset everyone if we don't conform. They assume we don't love them enough if we refuse to get them a gift. Basically, we have all our loved ones expecting something for a man-made holiday we purposefully stuffed full of expectations.

The same can be said of Christmas. How do you get your kids twenty presents from Santa based on toy store commercials and store displays showing dozens of presents under a tree? It's hard to tell your children that the store displays are really empty boxes wrapped in Christmas paper, or that those items need to be paid for in order to take them home.

It's become such a part of the social norm that when people tell us to just bring ourselves, or that they don't want any gifts, we feel uneasy. We end up bringing a dish just because it feels weird showing up empty-handed. We think that even if people don't imply it, they are still anticipating something—then we label it as a polite gesture.

HOW DO I ENJOY MYSELF GIVEN MY REALITY?

"People who are in good mental health come to terms with the reality of their situation and say, 'Screw it, I'm going to enjoy myself anyway.'"

~~~~~~~

Reality can be altered to a degree, but constantly forcing expectations that don't meet your reality is just going to lead to major frustration. Knowing when to accept reality or change it is probably one of the biggest obstacles to true happiness. For many of us, the lines become blurred. Yet finding joy is the difference between acknowledging what we want to happen and working around what is actually occurring.

We are told countless times that those in good mental health aren't the people you see on social media having all their expectations met. They aren't out there living the dream life. They are the people making the best out of whatever situation they happen to find themselves in at the time. They are working toward their dreams, but they know that achieving those goals won't necessarily cause instant bliss. They understand that true joy comes from making a choice. They find the power within themselves to be happy regardless of what's going on around them. They understand that no relationship will solve all their problems, no magic number of items or people will make them complete, and no set formula for life exists that will bring endless fulfillment. Happiness is a decision. It is a way of life that leads to joy.

Happy people are fully aware of the way this works, and they find a way to use what they have to their advantage. They find ways to have fun in their relationships even if there are going to be days where they argue. They bring the joy they already hold to the relationship; they don't let the relationship become their only source of happiness.

Likewise, happy people don't necessarily have to be at the top of their career. They find something about their jobs that they like to do that will get them through the day. They aren't expecting those jobs to fulfill them, but they carry joy with them into the office. They aren't waiting for their jobs to make them happy; they are making themselves happy despite having to work.

Basically, happy people learn that happiness is within their control. They aren't giving that power over to people, things, or circumstances that will eventually disappoint them. They may find joy in what they have in life, but they don't depend on those things to enjoy life. Joy is always the result of a choice they make and never the product of their circumstances.

Picture joy as a box. You are constantly putting in and taking items out of the box. Those items could be your relationship, friendships, quality time with family, your job, or a few hobbies. As you add these things to your box, you add to your joy. However, regardless of what's being added or taken out, the foundation of the box never changes. The box may be lighter as you remove things, but that doesn't stop it from being a box. It doesn't stop being what it is based on what's in it. It doesn't turn into a bag if you end some friendships or lose your job.

Even if the box is empty, that hope in a constant source tells you that the box is actually making room for other things when the time is right. So, you can still have joy despite what is going on in your life. Your joy doesn't have to change along with your circumstances—you just make the best out of what's in the box.

People who are in good mental health come to terms with this reality and say, "Screw it, I'm going to enjoy myself anyway." That means while everyone is complaining about the company picnic being held over the weekend, those people are usually the ones who find the fun in being with their coworkers outside of the office. They are getting to know each other and enjoying the BBQ, while you are off to the side mumbling about how you have to see everyone on Monday morning. You know this resonates because you all work at the same place and are obligated to attend the same function. It's not like anyone was excused from attending. Same situation, different outcome, all based on reality versus expectations.

This is not to say you shouldn't expect to receive things in life or give up on your dreams. In fact, we will discuss how you can prepare for realistic expectations in the next chapter. In this case, I'm talking about working around unrealistic expectations that we place on people or things to make us happy. Particularly, being unable to accept when things aren't going the way we would like them to occur. There is a huge difference between going after what you want, and trying to fit a circle into a square hole.

I'm a firm believer that dreams should be pursued. I also believe you should dream big. Having dreams that seem impossible doesn't necessarily mean they are unrealistic. So, by all means, tackle your goals. Just don't become disappointed when you have to be flexible in how you achieve them. Never equate being realistic to being complacent.

Chapter Four:

Paint Your Own Picture of Joy

> "It's not about sitting around waiting to feel good inside.
> It's about finding those things that make you feel good
> and then putting them into practice."

I've heard people say that you should create your own joy. However, I never like to use the term *create* because it sounds like I'm buying furniture that's marked "assembly required." I feel like I have to build that joy with no tools. It's almost as if someone is telling me, "Here are all the parts to joy, now good luck putting it together."

I also find it frustrating when someone implies that you need to spend tons of money to create that joy. The typical advice is to take an expensive vacation instead of feeling sorry for yourself. If the trip isn't down memory lane, chances are I can't afford it.

On the other hand, I believe that I can paint a picture of what happiness looks like to me, and then attempt to do the very things in that vision that bring me feelings of joy. I can use what I already have to experience joy, and then make it my responsibility to continue taking those actions that make me happy.

I think vision boards work well in this case. They aren't just for setting goals, but for maintaining happiness as well. You get a picture or snapshot of what makes you happy. You then set out to accomplish those goals or infuse them into your life. It doesn't have to feature only long-term goals, but short-term goals as well, such as spending an hour relaxing.

No assembly required.

Keep in mind that your picture of joy doesn't have to make everyone else happy; it should make you happy. My happiness could be watching my favorite reality show while tweeting about the episode. It could be listening to music and dancing around the house, or going on a walk so I can take in all the scenery. For someone else, it might be arts and crafts. Do what you think joy looks like for you given where you are in life. You may not have a job, but maybe that gives you free time to find a new show to watch to distract yourself from your employment status. It could be that you were working hard and didn't have the time to spend with family and friends. Now you have the time to plan activities with them that will help you reconnect.

I've learned that joy is something you have to work toward with each moment of happiness. Just like anything else in life, it's something you work at on a daily basis. Even when dealing with mental distress like depression, you can still choose to do some things that bring you joy. You can still start the day with the mentality that you will experience joy in some capacity.

It's not about sitting around waiting to feel good inside. It's about finding those things that make you feel good and then putting them into practice. You need to pick out some constructive, required activities that will bring you joy for the day.

Quit holding on to the assumption that joy is a permanent state of mind, when it's a habit you form over time. Just like brushing your teeth in the morning, you must get into a routine of finding joy. You develop that routine by preparing for joy in your life, learning from your pain, and releasing the things stopping you from experiencing true happiness.

PREPARING FOR JOY

**"You don't wait until you accomplish your
goal to celebrate;
you find reasons to rejoice until that goal is met."**

~~~~~~~~

In the last chapter, we discussed unrealistic expectations. This includes placing unreasonable demands on other people and things to make you happy. It also includes the refusal to be flexible in reaching your goals. Nonetheless, it's good to have dreams in mind that you can work toward. If those goals are realistic, then your next step should be preparing for joy to come your way. You don't wait for joy to find you. You must prepare yourself for the joy you have yet to receive. This means you don't wait until you accomplish your goal to celebrate; you find reasons to rejoice until that goal is met. It's called the journey to joy because you have to take many paths to get there. It doesn't happen overnight, and it doesn't negate the fact that there will be detours or setbacks. Life is not always about getting to your destination, but about enjoying the actual voyage it takes to get there.

For example, if you are single and want to be married, don't sit there wallowing in self-pity. Recognize that marriage is the destination. There is a trip you must take in order to get to that destination. So, start preparing yourself to be a good husband or wife. Read books or articles on marriage. Learn from the wisdom of those around you who are in solid marriages. Learn from those who have been divorced, so you don't make the same mistakes. You can even look into wedding décor and prices just for fun. By the time you are planning your wedding, you will know exactly what you want. You will enjoy not only the destination, but also the journey it took to get there. Ladies, just don't go out buying a wedding dress. I'm pretty sure that will scare potential partners away.

You can apply this idea to many goals in life. Want a new job? Work on perfecting your interview techniques. Brush up on the skills needed to do your dream job. Start networking so you can connect to other people in your field. For instance, if you want to be a teacher, connect with other educators. Want a better income? Stop thinking about what's currently in your bank account. Instead, look into financial planning, so you will know how to manage your money when it comes to you. That way, you are not splurging when your income finally increases.

My mom always wanted her own home. It took her years to buy one, but when she did she was ready to move in because she had bought dishes, towel sets, and even a welcome mat. She didn't sit around upset about not owning her own home; she made the necessary moves to become a homeowner. She looked into the housing market in various areas she wanted to live. She created a budget according to how much she would need as a down payment. I remember because we stopped ordering pizza every weekend. Instead, she started a savings account for emergencies, which proved effective when our hot water tank broke down months after we moved in.

I learned from my mom in my pursuit of a doctorate. Instead of getting discouraged, I would watch how my professors conducted themselves. I would attend and present at conferences. At those events, I would forget that I was a student because I presented myself as a professional. I studied everything I could get my hands on that dealt with my field. I ordered a stack of books on writing a dissertation long before I wrote one. I even practiced putting doctor in front of my name just to see how it would look on paper. In my mind, I already had a doctorate, so getting to graduation was only a matter of proving to the world why I should officially use the title. I had to start thinking like a doctor long before I became one.

I've learned that part of enjoying success is in the preparation. It's not about what you gain, but how prepared you are to handle what you've been given. Therefore, I often tell those who are looking to reach their goals to write them down. The Holy Bible suggests the idea that there is something powerful about writing down your vision. You are more likely to tackle those goals when you see them written down in front of you (versus just holding the thought in your mind). Once your goals are put on paper, you can start making steps towards achieving them. Looking at those goals will be a constant reminder to stay prepared for the joy that is yet to come.

LEARN FROM YOUR PAIN

"While the pain is real, the feeling of defeat is an illusion."

~~~~~~~

Everyone will endure pain at some point. It's just a fact of life. You can do everything right and still experience pain. You can do all that is in your power, and still have trouble. It's really the way we respond to our circumstances that makes all the difference. Regardless of what we are going through, we still have power. We have control over how we respond to those difficulties. If we choose to take on a defeated mentality, we double our pain. We end up enduring the pain of feeling defeated along with the pain brought on by our circumstances.

While the pain is real, the feeling of defeat is an illusion.

We feel defenseless. We feel like there is no way out. However, feelings aren't necessarily facts. I can feel broke but still be able to pay my bills on time. To someone who is unemployed, I wouldn't be broke at all. The truth is, you don't have to claim defeat, and you don't have to be the victim anymore. You are a survivor (or you wouldn't be reading this book right now). You have come this far, and you can keep going.

I never thought attitude had anything to do with the way I viewed life until I was forced to change it. I never saw pain as a strengthening experience, but a major inconvenience. I was very quick to take on that defeated, victim mentality because it rendered me powerless to change the situation. I never had to face the problem if I was too busy blaming everything or everyone else. I had no power over the situation because it was never my fault.

It didn't matter whether my hardships were out of my control or a result of my stubbornness; blaming gave me something to do with the pain without having to process it. As long as it wasn't my fault or responsibility, then I didn't have to move past acknowledging the hurt. I didn't have to evaluate my life and actually learn from the experience. If I was upset, it was usually because someone or something caused it. I never took the time to accept that being upset was my choice. I also never questioned why I chose to be upset as a response.

The older I get, the more I understand that pain has its purpose. We are so quick to question God or destiny when things get tough, but sometimes the only way for us to become better is to go through difficult times. It's not something we want to go through. No one wants to feel uncomfortable. No one wants to suffer. However, most people don't grow as individuals or figure out their purpose until they are up against the wall.

I think of pain as a signal, an indication that something needs to change for our own good. Physical pain tells us that something needs to be fixed within our bodies to make it better. Likewise, the emotional, mental, and spiritual pain we feel also forces us into necessary change for the better. It could be that we need to grow resistant, and we could not do that if we remain comfortable. It might be that our attitude needs to change, and we don't even recognize that we have a problem until that particular situation causes us to examine ourselves.

I thought I was a forgiving person until I was placed in hurtful situations where it seemed almost impossible to forgive. In every case, I had to make the choice to forgive whether or not I felt the person deserved it. Yet that process gave me a better understanding of grace and mercy. It made me reflect upon my own wrongdoings, hoping that those I offended would extend the same forgiveness I was trying to muster. I would've never understood that lesson if it were always easy to let things go. I would've missed the lesson altogether if I were too busy justifying my response by blaming everyone else.

I believe this is the key to finding joy in relationships. I didn't truly understand the definition of love until I was forced to extend it. I had to be pushed to the point of learning the beauty of love by having some pretty unlovable moments. Just like I realized I didn't know how to forgive until it became difficult for me to do so. Sometimes we have to go through some discomfort in order to get the message. Many of us actually stunt that growth by refusing to love or forgive others. We would much rather shield ourselves from the pain than learn the lesson behind it.

One thing I've learned about happiness is that the best way to stop agony is to learn from it. If pain is for a purpose, then I'm going to try my best to figure out that reason. If I'm sad, angry, or bitter, I'm going to find out what's making me feel that way. I take it as an opportunity to learn how to be a better person. I notice that many successful people take this same route when dealing with difficult situations.

It's hard to find one person doing well in life who didn't choose to learn from his or her hardships instead of wallowing in them. They always used those difficulties as a springboard to launch them into their destinies. You often read of celebrities or famous figures that were rejected multiple times before their careers took off. Where would they be if they decided to be bitter after a few rejections? What would happen if they decided to give up their dreams because of a few setbacks?

This is why I admire those who have dealt with mental distress. There is something about bouncing back from a troublesome time that lets you know just how strong you really are. If everything goes well, you can't gain the strength needed to overcome various challenges. It's almost like exercising. Those who lift weights may feel some discomfort, but they become stronger than the person who never stepped foot in the gym.

WHAT'S STEALING MY JOY?

Joy Drainers

"Truth be told, some people don't even like themselves, so what makes you think they will find the compassion needed to like you? If they can't stomach being their own best friend, what makes you think they can be yours?"

~~~~~~~

I'm learning to accept three facts when dealing with people who want to steal my joy:

1. Everyone will not like me.

2. Everyone will not agree with the things that I say or do.

3. Everyone is not on my team.

In a perfect world, everyone would love me. However, we live in an imperfect society where one slip-up or disagreement can cause strife. We live in a world where people would rather hate than love because loving others takes too much energy. We constantly run into people who are just plain unhappy in life and find it entertaining to make others feel just as miserable.

Listen, I would like to tell you that each person has goals and is working toward being their best selves. However, that's not true. Some people have no goals of their own, and they don't want you to have any either. Others want to add drama and negativity to your life because that's all they have to offer.

Some people don't want to improve and want to bring you into their mediocrity. They want their situations to stay the same even if the changes they would undergo are positive ones.

Chances are there's someone who hates your personality. Chances are you will encounter someone who finds every reason to disagree with you. Chances are you will find someone waiting for you to fail instead of cheering you on. You like to call them haters—anyone who tries to snatch the joy right from under you. I like to call them reality gauges. They allow me to take inventory of what I'm doing in life (or what I don't want to become). They remind me of reality: if everyone likes me, then I'm not doing my job.

If everyone loved me, then there would be a huge problem because that would mean I'm busy conforming to everyone's standards. Because everyone has a different opinion, successfully supporting all of those various opinions would be nearly impossible. I would be giving power to other people instead of taking on the freedom of being myself. At the point of being liked by everyone, I'm letting others dictate or approve of everything I believe, say, and do. It's like needing someone to sign your permission slip to go on a field trip.

The truth of the matter is that as long as you are making moves, you will have people who dislike you. If you were sitting around eating potato chips all day, then no one would care. There would be nothing to discuss. On the other hand, people will have something to talk about if you give them a reason. Let's use my book, for example. I'm writing this book with the understanding that some people will enjoy it, and some people won't like it at all. Some people may say they don't like it just because they find it enjoyable to debate with those who do. However, if I didn't write this book, there wouldn't be anything to hate.

You can't hate on nothing.

Basically, hating becomes obsolete if there isn't anything worthwhile to hate on.

You are worthwhile.

Therefore, you will have haters.

Try not to take it personally. Whether people like you or not is their problem. Whether they are hurt, wounded, angry, or bitter is none of your concern. That's something they need to face. It has nothing to do with you. Besides, you probably wouldn't be able to figure it out if you tried. Hate has no logic, so stop trying to reason with it.

Truth be told, some people don't even like themselves, so what makes you think they will find the compassion needed to like you? If they can't stomach being their own best friend, what makes you think they can be yours? As my mom would say, "Even Jesus had people who didn't like Him, and He was God ... so who are you to think that you won't come across the same problem?" According to Christianity, if the perfect person to ever walk the earth had people who hated Him just for being Himself, then it's safe to say you aren't exempt. They hated Him for being too nice, which goes to show you that even at your best, you can't please everyone.

Honestly, some people aren't meant to like you for whatever reason they can find—skin color, hair color, personality traits, your accomplishments, or simply because you prefer whole wheat over gluten-free bagels. It is what it is.

And then there are just certain people who you won't vibe with in the least. You won't get along with them nor see eye to eye; or their personality will clash with yours to the point of utter annoyance (and vice versa). At some point, you have to learn to find common ground, keep the peace as best as possible, and stay true to yourself. Don't change to conform to what people want you to be with the false assumption that everyone will accept you. That's not going to happen. And trust me, you don't want everyone to accept you. Sometimes, it's a blessing in disguise when someone wants nothing to do with you—the less people, the less drama, which gives you more room to focus your attention on those who appreciate you. So getting upset because someone doesn't like you is wasted effort. Surround yourself with those who are going to build you up instead.

Now that you know, the new rule is to simply not entertain those who dislike you.

From now on, stop making time for people who don't deserve it. If you keep talking and have a schedule to keep, you might as well put them on the agenda. Pencil them in on your calendar for that 8:00 a.m. appointment because that's what you are doing every time you disrupt your day for nonsense. Mentally, you are catering to their entertainment needs when you hand over time from your day just for them. Seriously, I want you to start keeping track of how much time you spend discussing your haters each week. Look at the number of hours. Now, imagine what you could do if you focused on something productive instead. I don't know about you, but I like to clear my calendar for those who are worth my time.

People Pleasing

"The day I found joy was the day I stopped listening to everyone's opinion of how I should or could live happily ever after."

~~~~~~~~

Finding things that bring you joy is hard enough. Now, you add to that having people telling *you* what will make *you* happy. How does that work? It really doesn't. Yet it happens every day.

The day I found joy was the day I stopped listening to everyone's opinion of how I should or could live happily ever after. I realized that everyone had a vision for my life and most of it didn't align with my idea of happiness. It takes a certain amount of courage to disengage from the expectations of others. When we are younger, we are told to go to school, get a job, and start a family. We are told that this is the dream life. So, we feel bad when we don't get that degree or hold a certain position. We feel bad when we aren't married or have two and a half kids. Yet it's liberating to find out that there is no white picket fence. You can paint that fence any color you want ... and no one should tell you otherwise.

The good news is that many people want the best for you. The bad news is that many people want the best for you. They have good intentions behind seeing you do well, but you may not like the picture they paint of the best life. Yet we let other people tell us why we should pick a certain major, why we should settle for a certain job, why we should or shouldn't marry, or why we need to have kids by a certain time. We let people schedule the activities and events in our lives like we're an experiment. It's as if we let people tell us what to do just to see if it works. Then, if it doesn't make us happy, we are stuck with the consequences.

Many of us are unhappy because we're resentful. We resent following the directions of others. We wish we had gone left when everyone told us we would be much happier going right.

We really have to step back and realize that most of the problems we face rest in our inability to separate our happiness from everyone else's version of happiness. We have to separate what we want in life from what others have in store for us. We end up trying to make other people happy as they look in on our lives. However, living out the life they picked for us is straight misery.

Yes, everyone else is happy about the job, but they don't have to clock in every morning. Everyone is happy they were able to attend a wedding with free food, drinks, and dancing, but they don't have the job of maintaining the relationship after the tables are cleared. Everyone is so excited when there's a baby, but no one is willing to babysit.

So, stop letting other people tell you how to be happy!

People who are forcing you to be happy on their own terms aren't helping you; they are stealing your joy. The more time you spend making them happy, the less time you have to find your own peace of mind. Ironically, to get peace, you are going to have to upset some people.

Sorry. That's just the way things work.

If your life is making everyone happy, then you are doing something wrong. Chances are, if everyone else is happy, then it's at your expense. The more people you try to please, the more freedom you lose—your life becomes more about making other people happy instead of enjoying yourself.

Let's be clear. It's nice to go out of your way to make someone happy. The problem is when you make a lifestyle out of it. The problem occurs when you are so focused on not offending others that you don't have time to actually live your life. It's nice that you keep other people in mind when going about your day, but some decisions that are better for you are going to upset at least one person you know.

You can't please everyone all the time. Some people are going to be happy, and others are going to be disappointed. None of that matters. The main thing that matters is that *you* are happy. If you are happy, then facing those disappointed people won't be as difficult. You are too busy enjoying your life to want to go about it any other way.

We live in misery because we are scared of hurting others. We are afraid of hurting someone's feelings. We feel guilty because everyone doesn't approve. We don't want to upset the balance we have in our relationships, friendships, family, and on and on.

So many of us are living other people's lives, which is redundant since they are also living their lives without your input. Someone is getting the benefit of leading two different lives—theirs and ours—but we end up with the short end of the stick.

I must make it clear that you will *never* get everyone's approval for everything you do. I don't care what decision is being made. It can be something as simple as making a purchase. Some people may agree, and some people will say you don't need it. However, when it comes to life-changing decisions, their approval isn't necessary. They have the right to voice their opinion. You are given the option to choose to listen. However, the final decision is up to you.

If I had decided not to move 10 hours away from home to complete my PhD, I would have missed my purpose entirely. Of course, some people didn't want me to leave. I'm sure some people didn't believe me when I said I was moving. Others didn't understand or thought I was making the wrong decision. I made the final decision to move because I felt it was needed. I didn't have the energy to explain why it was necessary. I didn't have the time to convince multiple people that it was the best move for me. I was too focused on my goal to feel guilty.

So, let me ask you, how many people are you willing to

make happy at the expense of your wellbeing? A few? A dozen? Everyone you meet?

You must understand that people have their own picture of joy. Don't let them paint yours.

Taking on Other People's Problems

"Don't punish yourself for the mistakes of others."

~~~~~~~

My former pastor once told me that I was unhappy because I was stressed out from taking on other people's issues. He said, "If it doesn't have your name on it, then don't pick it up." This doesn't mean you shouldn't help others. By all means, volunteer, provide advice, or help someone through a difficult time. However, don't punish yourself for the mistakes of others.

If someone you know decided to blow off getting a good job, don't beat yourself up trying to pay their expenses. That is their problem and not yours. If someone wants to date people who make him or her miserable, please don't take on their misery as if you're the one in the relationship.

People have to take responsibility for their own actions. People have to accept the reality of the choices they make. Sometimes, there are no do-overs. You can't press the reset button. Yet you are constantly being that reset button in their lives. You do this by saving them from the consequences. As a result, they never learn how to do things differently because they are expecting you to help them each time they make a mistake. Then you end up taking on the burden as if you are the one making those errors. Everyone loses.

One piece of advice that helped me with this realization was just accepting the fact that I am not God. I am not able to take on everyone's issues and still manage my own problems. I just can't. That's not to sound mean; it's just reality. People make poor choices. People decide to live with those poor choices. Sometimes, they actually enjoy living that way.

Often, individuals end up in unfortunate situations. I'm not talking about when someone falls on hard times. I'm talking about when people make a living out of not helping themselves, while expecting others to constantly be there to pick up the slack. They make you think that they can't make it without you, but they are using you.

You see, human beings are all about survival. If you don't help them, they will find someone else who will. It's just that you seem to be the one who is most willing to jump in and save them. So, they come to rely on you. It's nice to be a help, but at some point it becomes harmful behavior. You become burnt out and unhappy for taking on all their burdens, and they can't figure out other solutions besides reaching out to you.

It's the catch-22 of enabling destruction.

As long as people are comfortable with you dragging them out of their circumstances, they will remain in that situation. There is no need for them to change. You don't have to force them out of their comfort zones. You cosign their behavior by telling them it's okay because you have everything under control. Yet the problem itself is out of control on both ends.

I stopped taking on problems with the realization that God or the universe has a way of teaching people lessons that are critical to success in life. If you get in the way of that, you mess up the natural rhythm of helping that person get ahead. If you are constantly stepping in with the solution, those people never learn how to truly solve the issue on their own. They never seek out the resources to handle themselves without you. They become dependent.

Dependency leads to expectations.

Expectations you can't meet cause stress.

That's why you are stressed out.

Help others, but know when to draw the line.

Feeling Guilty for Saying No … Feeling Bitter for Saying Yes

"Even if your plan is to stay at home all day eating snacks and taking naps, then that's your plan for the day. Whether they like those plans is none of your concern."

~~~~~~~

No. No. No. It's still hard for me to say. I even feel guilty telling telemarketers I'm not interested in buying their products.

For many of us, there's usually a sense of guilt behind the word "no." That's because people don't like rejection, and we don't want to be the one doing the rejecting. Simply put, people hate being told that they can't get what they want. There is a natural conflict when you tell them what they don't want to hear. This is especially true if they don't understand why. They think an automatic "yes" is in order if they took the time to ask.

However, as an adult, you don't need to explain to others why you refuse to follow through on their requests. If they aren't paying your bills, they shouldn't care about what you are doing with your time. Therefore, if they want you to plan the first gathering of the year, they will just have to be upset when you say you can't do it. Even if your plan is to stay at home all day eating snacks and taking naps, then that's your plan for the day. Whether you tell them your original plans is optional. Whether they like those plans is none of your concern.

However, respecting that decision is a requirement.

More than likely, it will frustrate them that they will either have to find someone else, do it themselves, or scratch the idea altogether. That frustration makes people go to extreme lengths to get a reply from you. They will beg or plead with you; they may downsize the amount of energy, time, or effort it will take to get it done. They will do whatever it takes for you to reconsider.

This is where we usually give in and say, "Oh, okay. Fine."

Then our guilt turns to bitterness. We sit there saying, "I can't believe I have to do this event," or "They made me run all these errands." No they didn't. You better start believing because you just made yourself do those things. The person only had to make you feel uncomfortable enough to give in. Yet giving in was your choice. You could have said you were going to the movies that day instead, yet you didn't voice that as an option. You said you would do it. Therefore, you aren't necessarily mad at the task itself, but the fact that you gave in to their demands.

You need to understand that you made the decision to take on the responsibility. You need to own that. Then, you need to decide how you will respond next time. My suggestion is don't make any promises, take time to think things through before making a decision, and to be realistic about what you can handle. Of course, if it's going to make you miserable, opt out immediately. You aren't obligated to say "yes" to anything right away.

You have the ability to tell that person that you will think it over or that you can't make any promises at the moment. Don't commit to something that will make you bitter in the end. You will be more resentful when you find out that there were other people on the call list that would have been happy to do it. You will be upset when that person's response is, "Well, you didn't have to do it."

You have options, so start using them.

Chapter Five:

Prepare for Emotional Roadblocks

> *"Emotions are not a buffet where you can pick and choose what you want to feel."*

One fact that literally changed my life:

Emotions come as a packaged deal.

Emotions are not a buffet where you can pick and choose what you want to feel. In fact, they often work together. Imagine you are picking a color to paint your living room. You look at all the reds and you feel disappointed; you look at the shades of green and feel rather nonchalant. You look at the blues and feel a sense of excitement. The different shades of blue make you extremely content. You decide that blue is the best color for your room.

However, you wouldn't truly know how happy you were with the color blue unless you experienced the feelings for the colors that didn't make you happy. In fact, you are more confident and satisfied with the color you chose because of all the feelings of dissatisfaction you felt without it. If the only choice you had was the color blue, then you might not appreciate it or even know how happy it made you—you have nothing to compare it with.

Let me ask you some questions: How would you know what it felt like to be excited if you never felt disappointed? How would you know what it's like to be content if you never took the time to understand how you respond to being discontent? Joy comes in the same package. You can't pick up joy and leave sadness behind. In fact, the key to really feeling joy comes from comparing it to the times that weren't so joyful. Being sad makes you appreciate being happy. Being uncomfortable makes you appreciate comfort all the more.

It's like dating. You make the decision to settle down with someone based on what you want in a relationship *after* you've experienced what you don't want (although some of us continue to stay in relationships that we don't want, but that's a different story for another book).

The issue is that so many of us hate being uncomfortable that we want to pick up all the positive emotions and leave the negative ones. However, when you throw one away, you throw away the other. When you decide not to understand why you are sad, then you will remain sad. When you actually accept that sometimes people are upset, you can learn what it takes to make you happy. Your emotions work together as one system.

This is why it's troubling to see so many people ignore their mental health. We run from negative emotions to the point where people are ashamed for feeling them. We think all we should feel are positive emotions. If any negative emotions appear, we think something is wrong with us. It's not fair that those in distress have to feel guilty because everyone else pretending to be okay wants to feel a false sense of comfort. If you aren't suffering in silence or ignoring the problem like they are, then you aren't being strong enough. Unfortunately, the only thing we become stronger at is pretending those emotions don't exist. It doesn't take away the pain, but rather suppresses it. Then it manifests in unhealthy ways like in what we eat, the habits we develop, and the way in which we see ourselves.

There is a saying I always refer to when people talk about seeking help or support: the people who need therapy rarely get the help, while the people in therapy are there to learn how to deal with the people who refuse to go. There are those who think they are crazy because they decided to ask for help. Yet most of their time in therapy is spent trying to gain the coping skills to deal with the unresolved issues of the people around them who also need therapy. You will often hear therapists say that the person who really needs to be in the room is hardly ever present.

People can talk about those going to therapy all they want, but it's probably one of the smartest things one can do for their own wellbeing. I believe that everyone, to some degree, has problems they are struggling with on a daily basis—some are just better at hiding it than others. Even the fact that some choose to stay in denial by thinking they can handle things on their own, or refuse to admit they have an issue altogether is a problem. Some are out there mocking those who seek help, but they are one incident short of a mental breakdown. There are those who talk about the behavior of others but don't realize people are questioning their behavior. No one is perfect, and if someone says they are, then they are lying.

Just because you decline the offer to get help doesn't negate the fact that you need it. Just because you've managed to avoid making an appointment doesn't change the fact that one may be in order. And just because you've been able to somewhat function doesn't prove that the problem doesn't exist. It's like tricking yourself into believing you aren't that bad at math because you refuse to hire a tutor. Then you laugh at those who actually have tutors because, for some strange reason, they want to get better. Meanwhile, there are still some problems you can't solve (pun intended).

We need to learn how to take responsibility for managing our emotions or we will never be happy. We also need to stop letting other people (who also have issues) dictate how we go about getting support. Who are they to talk when they probably need just as much help? Think about it.

HOW DO I MANAGE MY EMOTIONS?

"One of the reasons we find it hard to manage our emotions is that we don't plan for them. We don't accept that they will come. We don't accept that something will need to be done when they arrive."

~~~~~~~

Managing your emotions can be done with the following steps:

1. Awareness

2. Acknowledgement

3. Acceptance

4. Action

Awareness begins with educating yourself on mental health issues and concerns. There are a number of resources that will help you learn about mental health, address various questions and concerns, and provide support. Those resources are also helpful if you are thinking about therapy or social support groups. There are even support groups for those affected by a loved one's mental illness.

You may be asking, "How do I know the difference between having the blues and experiencing depression?" To distinguish between minor mental health concerns and a mental disorder, you must be aware of the criteria and warning signs that can indicate depression and other mental illnesses. Experiencing any or a combination of those symptoms for two weeks or more may indicate a mental disorder.

Please note that while there are other symptoms specific to severe mental disorders, such as schizophrenia that include hallucinations, this book focuses on common mental disorders such as depression and anxiety. These are most frequent in society, are highly treatable (yet most people don't get help due to the stigma or shame), and affect millions. Specifically, the National Alliance on Mental Illness (NAMI) reports 16 million adults having one depressive episode in the past year. Therefore, it's important to be aware of some of the warning signs for various forms of depression and anxiety. For a complete list, visit the National Alliance on Mental Illness (NAMI) at www.nami.org.

Warning Signs For Adults	Warning Signs For Children
Feeling excessively sad or low	Excessive worry or fear
Mood changes (may include feelings of euphoria or uncontrollable high)	Frequent temper tantrums
Difficulty thinking or concentrating	Changes in school performance
Irritability or anger	Frequent disobedience and aggression
Problems sleeping (too much or not enough)	Frequent nightmares
Feeling tired or having low energy	Hyperactive activity
Avoiding friends, family or social activities	Fighting against bedtime

Warning Signs For Adults	Warning Signs For Children
Inability to carry out daily activities	Fighting against going to school
Multiple physical ailments or aches (Headache, stomachache)	
Changes in eating habits	
Thoughts of suicide	

Source: National Alliance on Mental Illness

While it's good to be aware of mental health concerns, we also need to be aware of our emotions. This may seem like common sense. Yet it's not so easy considering the amount of people who are experts at suppressing their moods. As a result, it becomes difficult to describe what we are feeling and why. We live in a society where "I feel some type of way" is not just a saying, but a new term used when we can't specifically express ourselves. Being aware means we learn what makes us tick. We learn what gets us down. We learn what we can do to change those emotions.

Once we are aware of the problem, we must acknowledge it. We must be willing to admit that we are feeling down or upset. We must admit that we are anxious. We must acknowledge our emotions so that we can fully accept what is taking place. Once we accept that this is an emotion we are facing, then we can come up with constructive ways to allow those emotions to slide right on by. This teaches us to recognize negative emotions, but not to the extent that we stay stuck in a negative state.

Depression can be biological, but it can also occur when we brush off our feelings for too long. We don't acknowledge or accept our emotions long enough to take action. In some cases, we don't even get to the awareness stage because we pretend nothing is wrong. As a result, we allow our feelings to get so out of control that we can't handle them anymore. We like to deny how we feel, which causes us to ignore the pain until it's almost unbearable. If we are sad, then we should be okay admitting that. When we accept that sadness, we can begin to understand why.

For instance, maybe I'm angry with a friend because she never takes the time to visit me. If I'm not aware of or refuse to acknowledge the fact that I'm angry, then I'm more than likely going to stay that way. I will find myself becoming angry whenever the thought of my friend crosses my mind. It occurs so much that it becomes a habit. I don't even realize I'm angry. I tell myself that it doesn't bother me, although deep down it hurts.

If I finally take the time to admit that I'm angry and why, I have a better chance of controlling that anger. It allows me to be proactive rather than reactive in that I can mentally prepare myself when I'm dealing with that friend. I can expect that feeling to come when that friend doesn't show up. Then I can say to myself, "I had a feeling they would be a no show. That's why I planned to go to the mall as a back-up plan. I can still have a good time." Although I'm upset, I can control that feeling by incorporating activities to help me deal with the stress before I become too angry to do anything. The same works with depression, anxiety, disappointment, despair, etc.

Managing our emotions comes from being aware of them so we have a plan in place to tackle each emotion as it occurs. This is why it's good to create a tracking journal and a safety plan so we can monitor our moods (see Chapter 9 and 10). These tools give us a way of coming up with solutions before the problem becomes too much to bear. Often, we find it hard to manage our emotions because we don't plan for them. We don't accept that they will come. We don't accept that something will need to be done when they arrive. We get so caught up in our feelings when there is no need to do so.

In fact, getting so caught up in our feelings means our emotions are already out of control. However, if this does occur, we need an emergency plan to get them under control again. It's all about planning and preparation.

The rule is: Learn how to take control of your emotions before they take control of you.

HOW DO I HELP SOMEONE THROUGH A DIFFICULT TIME?

"We say 'snap out of it' until it's our turn to figure out how to do the snapping. We say 'just get over it' until we are forced to try it. We find it really easy to tell someone to pray it away until we are the ones doing the praying."

~~~~~~~

I've helped countless people simply because I tried to understand their pain instead of dismissing it. I don't go with the typical cliché lines that others use to cheer someone up. When it's hard to sympathize we say those things because they're such an easy response. It doesn't matter whether or not one can actually put those clichés into action. For instance, I often refrain from using the term "too blessed to be stressed." What does that mean? Does that mean I will never stress out because I'm blessed? Does that mean Christians can't have mental health concerns? What are the steps needed to become so blessed that I don't have to face any trials that will stress me out?

Saying those common remarks sounds good, but it doesn't validate feelings. It doesn't encourage that person to get help in dealing with those feelings. When interacting with people who are hurting, you must remember that the pain they feel clouds their judgment. All they want is acknowledgement of that pain. Actually, all they can process is the fact that you understand. Therefore, any comment that diminishes that pain will possibly be ignored. You don't want them shutting you out. You don't want them pretending to nod in agreement while thinking "they just don't get it."

You can choose to take action and sincerely pray for or with that person. However, saying "too blessed to be stressed" is a brush off. It falls under "snap out of it" or "get over it." It implies that one is too blessed to have the pain he or she is going through. To someone in mental distress, it sounds like, "I'm not blessed enough, so it must be wrong to feel this pain." Now you've just added guilt on top of hurt.

My mom, a very wise woman, once said, "No one will understand what you are going through until it affects them." She's right. We live in a society where people just don't care until they are faced with that issue. You see, empathy occurs when we've actually been in the other person's shoes. If the roles were reverse, what would we want to hear? Would you want someone saying "get over it" or you are "too blessed to be stressed" while you are in agony? So, why say it to someone else?

We say "snap out of it" until it's our turn to figure out how to do the snapping. We say "just get over it" until we are forced to try it. We find it really easy to tell someone to pray it away until we are the ones doing the praying.

We have to get past the cliché lines and start listening to those in pain. We have to make it a point to really be present. This means we must be in tune to their needs and know how to respond accordingly. Thus, I've put together this handy list of dos and don'ts filled with common responses for effective communication when dealing with someone in distress.

Do	Don't	Reasoning
Call to check in on them	Forget to call	Talking may be all that's needed
Be patient	Tell them to "get over it"	Feelings don't just go away on command
Pray for/with them	Tell them prayer is all they need	Treatment may be necessary
Mention the impact they have on your life	Get angry and come down on them	Knowing they're not a burden helps
Plan an easy activity	Get upset when they don't feel like hanging out	Activities are helpful, but don't make them tasks
Acknowledge what they are doing right	Say they need to do more	Mental distress is exhausting
Allow them to express their feelings	Say things could be worse	Feelings aren't validated which leads to guilt
Focus on the problem at hand	Tell them they should be grateful for what they have	One can be grateful and still feel pain
Contact a Crisis or Suicide hotline	Ignore warning signs	This is a cry for help

Chapter Six:

Identify Yourself as Valuable

> *Value (noun): the regard that something is held to deserve; the importance; worth, or usefulness of something.*

If you type in the word "value" in the Google search engine, you will find the definition above.

Therefore, by definition being valuable means one must be:

1. Deserving

2. Important

3. Worthy

4. Useful

We fit the criteria, we just don't believe we do. We don't believe so because unhealthy family or romantic relationships, friendships, society, or just plain jerks have told us otherwise.

You must know that your value doesn't change just because some people don't see your worth. I always go with the story of the hundred dollar bill. If you crumple or ball up a hundred dollar bill, it's still worth one hundred dollars. You wouldn't throw it in the trash because it had creases. You would smooth out that bill and be thankful you have a hundred dollars to spend. If some people don't see the worth of a hundred dollars, then that's their problem.

The same is true with you. You may have some people telling you how little you are worth. They crumble and ball you up to make it appear that you're worthless. In reality, they are the ones missing your value. The truth is that you are priceless.

Think about it.

No matter how people treat you or talk to you.

No matter whether you get that job or not.

No matter what's in your bank account.

No matter the number of people you call friends.

You are still priceless.

Your value doesn't decrease because someone else refuses to see your worth. Often, it's a matter of people having an issue seeing their value that causes the problem. If they can't see the value in themselves, then it's nearly impossible for them to see the value in others.

Nevertheless, you are not a used car. Whether you're parked in the lot to be admired, or someone drives off content with her decision, you as a human being DO NOT change in value. You are still worth so much more than you give yourself credit.

I hate that society tries to put a price on us based on our "success." We say, "Oh, he's worth a billion dollars." No. His income happens to be a billion dollars. That is the amount of money in his bank account at the time. As an individual, there's no price attached. Similarly, we see a single, beautiful woman and we say, "Why are you single? No one sees how beautiful you are or how much you are worth?" When did being in a relationship determine our worth? Does that mean the days you decide to go out on a date are your "worthy" days?

Truth be told, you go into a relationship with value, and you decide to leave or stay with that same value. Either way, there isn't a price attached. This isn't a sale. You're not an item on the sales rack. You might have sold yourself short with who you let into your life, but you sold yourself short of priceless. Huge difference.

HOW DO I ACCEPT MYSELF?

"We all start out with our own definition of self-worth, and someone or something comes along and tells us our definition is wrong."

~~~~~~~

We need to take a step back and look at the root cause of why we feel the way we do about ourselves. It may be painful, but it's necessary. It's okay to not be okay. It's not okay to pretend. Even if it's subconsciously, the things people say to us are going to reshape our definition of value. We all start out with our own definitions of self-worth, and someone or something comes along and tells us our definition is wrong, that we aren't worthy, deserving of great things, or important to our loved ones and society. That is a lie. Just the fact that we are human beings means that even at the basic level, we are deserving of essential needs. We are worthy enough to end up on this planet. We must be here for a reason. The sole miracle of being born is a sign that we are important to those whose paths we cross and to the society in which we are placed.

I think that good self-esteem and self-worth are the foundations of mental health. How you feel and what you believe about yourself will come across in your actions. Those prone to depression often have low self-esteem or self-worth that continuously says they are not worthy of love or care. That is simply not true. We are all valuable. We can all give and show love. We can all care about others and receive care in return. However, mental distress clouds our judgment so that we can only think of the negatives (and they aren't even true).

I don't care what someone has told you. God says otherwise. The universe says otherwise. Destiny's job in putting you on this planet is one meant to be fulfilled and not thrown away because of others.

I've had my share of experiences where my definition of value changed. Over time, I learned that others should never determine my value or worth. It should always align with the positive thoughts I hold about myself. You must do the same.

You must define your worth for yourself and stick with the value you know to be true over what others have to say.

The positive things people say about you are called compliments.

The negative things people say about you are called criticisms (even if they throw in the word "constructive").

Neither one determines who you are and what you state about your self-worth.

Compliments are nice, and criticisms are suggestions in which you need to consider the source. You can say "thank you for your kind remarks" or "thank you for your opinion," respectively. Regardless, your self-esteem stays the way you want it.

I was once told that if you rely too much on the compliments or criticisms of others, you put yourself in a vulnerable position. Those people have the ability to make you feel like a superstar and then make you feel like crap all in the same sentence. Don't put much weight into those reviews because the person telling you this isn't perfect either, and pleasing society is like trying to win an endless battle—it's exhausting.

Therefore, you decide who you are, and let no one change or try to define you. Let no one make you think you aren't worthy. Forget the standards people or society have placed on you. Create your own definition of what you bring to the world and stick with it. Only add to that definition if what is being said about your worth is positive and uplifting. If it's negative, throw it in the trash.

WHAT'S HURTING MY SELF-ESTEEM?

Comparing Myself to Others

"I like to call us the Photoshop culture. If we can Photoshop our pictures, then we are doing the same with our life events."

~~~~~~~

The best way to ruin your self-esteem is by comparing yourself to others. That's because if you look hard enough, you will find someone doing better than you at some point. The odds of finding someone doing well at something are extremely high. So, those odds are never in your favor. On any given day, you will find someone out of your 400 friends on social media who will announce that they just received a job offer, or that they are engaged, or that they are expecting. On the contrary, there are some people envious of your life right now. It's a game of disappointment that can go on and on if you let it.

You will see wedding and vacation photos. Then, as you are looking at them, you will wonder why you can't have a great job, family, and dream wedding, too. If you step back, you will notice that the person you are comparing yourself to is having one major life event (one that maybe you are still waiting to happen in your own life). You, on the other hand, took that one life event and became frustrated about *every* aspect of your life. This means that the person you are comparing yourself to might not be as happy as you think. That person may be starting that new job, but that's the best she had to share. You might not have a great job, but you could have a family. You may have time to go on vacation and post your own pictures. You may not have a wedding coming up, but you may have a better job compared to the person getting married.

You also don't know the backstory to those announcements. I stopped comparing myself to others when everything I was jealous of happened to look better on social media than it did when the person talked about it in real life. It's astonishing; most people put only the positives on their profile page. I like to call us the Photoshop culture. We Photoshop our pictures, then we do the same with our life events. We remove some parts of the story, highlight other moments, then minimize or leave out the bad parts altogether. In fact, for some people, posting positive messages is actually hopeful confirmation. Either it's for self-confirmation or in the hope that their happiness will be confirmed by the support of those who comment. If enough people believe you, then you can convince yourself that everything is cool.

It's pretty confusing because you will find that sometimes what's really going on is the exact opposite of what's being posted. We get upset because we think people are having this great life.

We think they have found joy in those things, and it depresses us.

While it's great to keep in contact via social media, we have to keep things in perspective. Otherwise, we will get sucked into believing that everyone's life is grand except our own.

Refusing to Forgive

"I didn't forgive to show the world that what they did was okay, but rather that I was okay with letting it go."

~~~~~~~~

A huge part of our self-esteem and self-worth is tied to our inability to forgive. This can be toward others and ourselves. This creates self- blame, and that shows up in how we treat ourselves. We need to see the situation for what it is and why we shouldn't fall for it.

First, if you need help forgiving, keep in mind that those who hurt you are already miserable (whether they want to admit it or not). It's the basic idea that hurt people, hurt people. People say you aren't cool and you believe them. Then you walk around feeling uncool to the point where you want others to feel that way as well. The hurt just keeps going.

Those who really know me are aware that I've been through some pretty horrible ordeals, situations in which it would seem that I had every right not to forgive. Yet I chose to forgive for my own peace of mind—not because I condoned the person's behavior. It wasn't to brush off what the person did. I didn't forgive to show the world that what they did was okay, but rather that I was okay with letting it go.

I often hear people say, "I can never forgive him or her for what they did to me." Well, yes, forgiveness is hard. However, living with bitterness is far worse. Walking around feeling bad is more debilitating. I understand how difficult it is to forgive, mainly because our self-esteem gets shattered, and, as a result, we have major trust issues to solve before we can move forward with another person. We open ourselves up to others and they betray us. This betrayal can occur in families, friendships, and relationships. So, how do we move past it?

1. Forgive Yourself

Someone once reminded me that you should forgive yourself first for your past decisions. Don't continue to feel guilty about decisions made when you were young and didn't understand the extent of what you were doing. You can't judge yourself to-day based off things that happened years ago. Today you know more. Otherwise, you wouldn't have the wisdom to judge your past actions or reactions. So stop blaming yourself for being a typical teenager or young adult. In the same regard, don't let others make you feel guilty. If you screwed up, then that's just part of the growing process. That doesn't mean you should go out there doing any and everything, but it does mean you have to give yourself a break when you look back and say, "Wow, that was a really bad decision." Don't let your past make you think less of yourself today. Instead, use it as a lesson for the future.

2. Understand that Everyone Holds Pain

You must also understand that the people who hurt you did so because they were also busy making their own mistakes. They probably had things going on in their lives that upset them. You just happened to be the person on whom they took out their frustrations. Everyone holds pain, and that pain manifests in various forms.

For example, people who are violent or abusive hold anger issues usually derived from needing some type of control to feel better or to define themselves. At some point, they felt out of control or helpless, and the easiest way to regain that sense of power is by controlling someone else. It's a way of deflecting from their insecurities.

Therefore, never blame yourself for being put in an abusive situation. No matter how it looks from the outside, you can't take the blame for being hurt. Some people are very good manipulators. If you were hit or talked to negatively on your first date, chances are you wouldn't call that person back. Yet it's hard to figure out what's going on when that person has gained your trust after years of being a sweetheart. Get help if you are trying to get out of an abusive situation.

3. Remember that Family Isn't Excluded from Feeling Pain

Unhealthy relationships with family cause stress not only because the same level of trust applies, but also because you are often tied to each other without a choice in the matter. History and connection makes it hard to receive criticism, much less accept harmful behavior. It's much easier to take negativity from someone you don't know versus someone you do (and should respect to a certain degree). It's also hard when the history you have with that person makes you feel guilty for having to remove yourself if you are unable to make amends.

Sometimes you aren't able to completely remove yourself from the situation. You will see that person at Christmas or the next family reunion. In this situation, remember our realistic expectations. Is it possible that you can work things out? Is it possible that you can distance yourself? Are you able to get to a point where you can be cordial during family functions even if you don't see each other in between?

If the relationship is destructive or abusive, you most definitely have to step back or set boundaries. I don't care what title people hold; if they can't respect you, then you need to put yourself in a position where you feel comfortable dealing with them. If you have to deal with that person from a distance, then so be it. In other situations, you decide what you choose to deal with and when. If you're getting nagged at Thanksgiving dinner, you could possibly muster up the strength to let it go for that one day. However, at some point, you have to determine the people you let into your inner circle, be they family or friends. If they don't make the list, then they just don't make the list. Love them from afar.

You must also take into account that just because you spend more time with family or because they are relatives doesn't excuse them from the same troubles as anyone else you meet. They still have a story. They still experience pain, and they can still dump their pain onto you just like anyone else. If you think you know their story because you are part of the same family, then guess again. Chances are you don't know everything. So, the fact that they are members of your family doesn't mean there aren't issues that they are dealing with that may affect their ability to love, care, or respect others.

We tend to hold extremely high expectations for family out of a sense of loyalty. We expect them to be perfect. When they fall short, it's more personal in nature than a fallout with a random friend or an encounter with a stranger on the street. However, your family members are still human beings with flaws. This doesn't give them the right to disrespect you. However, given the case, it does mean that you shouldn't come down on them any harder than someone else making the same mistakes.

I understand history can make this difficult for some, mainly because family has the habit of bringing up old mistakes. I know using past mistakes or knowledge to hurt others can be done in any type of relationship, but I acknowledge this under family because it is where people seem to experience it the most. It comes down to this: those who think they know you have a hard time letting go. They still hold on to the mentality that you are the same person making the same mistakes you made years ago. Either that, or they want to stunt that growth by constantly reminding you of your past. They realize that keeping you focused on prior errors or circumstances distracts you from doing better or moving forward.

Even if they don't know the full story, it's a way of telling someone who they are based on past events so they will never evolve. Either out of comfort, revenge, intimidation, or jealousy, somehow, in their mind, they refuse to acknowledge your growth. Sometimes, when you have been around people long enough, it may be hard to recognize the changes they have made over time. In their mind, you are probably the same person you were in 2005 versus present day. However, the simple fact that they have to go that far back in time to hurt you shows where they are mentally—they are stuck in the past.

Regardless of the situation, you need to be aware that the past is over. It's done. The more you defend your past, the more time you waste in the present. Ultimately, that stagnation affects your future. You are not the same person you were even a year ago. It's called maturity. If one's mentality hasn't changed over the years, then something is wrong. So, while others may struggle with moving on, that doesn't mean you have to stay there with them.

4. Keep in Mind that Everyone Can't be a Friend

Before we get upset at the people in our lives, we need to take a quick look at what it takes to be a friend. We need to be realistic in terms of how many people can truly meet those requirements. Then we need to stop giving people titles they can't earn. I believe most friendships don't last because, as you grow older, being a friend becomes harder. There is a certain amount of effort when you start taking on the true definition of friendship.

Loyalty takes effort.

In first grade, it's easy to say that someone is your best friend just because you want someone to call your best friend. However, when you are 25, friendship becomes more than the title itself. You may have to sit with that person for hours on end, drive to their house when they need help, or help them out financially when you see them going through a tough time.

When I was in grade school, I had a whole table of best friends. My grandma would always correct me and say they were not my friends, they were my associates. I didn't know what associates meant at the time, so she told me to just start referring to everyone as my classmate. She was right. Most turned out to be people I happened to take classes with at the time.

Now, I have a best friend and a few close friends I've met over the years, perhaps maybe five in total. I hear younger kids complaining about not having friends. I know it means a lot at the time, but when you are older you will be thankful you have what they call "4 quarters instead of 100 pennies." You will learn it's not the quantity, but the quality of your friends that counts.

Social media makes this concept difficult because your reputation is based on how many people are on your friends list, how many likes you get, or how many people follow you. Yet most of those people don't even know you. They probably don't even know your favorite color. So, you can't count on all 400 of your friends to back you. You are still counting on the same few people you deal with when you sign off. It's not a measure of your worth. In fact, it's even better when you clean your friends list down to people you are close with or who actually know you in some capacity.

I was able to forgive many of my "friends" when I came to terms with the fact that they were not friend material. I realized that not everyone was meant to be my friend. You can't take everyone with you on your journey. You may have to leave some people behind. Everyone's luggage won't fit in the car, and the weight of that baggage is only going to hold you back. The main thing to remember when wondering why certain friendships didn't make the list is that maybe they weren't meant to make the cut. They may make someone else's list, but they don't fit the criteria to tag along on yours.

5. Don't Let Others Drag You into their Misery

People who are negative or jealous toward you are miserable because your character forces them to examine themselves. Bullies and haters take advantage of your good nature. They can be upset for being unable to uphold the same character traits they envy in you. They realize you are able to receive the love they crave, so they try to upset that balance so you can also be miserable and feel unloved. This is why I say you have to keep your self-esteem based on how you feel. It's very easy for people to make you think negative thoughts about yourself when the problem is with them.

They may also be jealous of you because your success forces them to take a good look at what they are doing in life. The more you do, the more they question why they aren't doing the same. They may be resentful because you took the risk or had the courage to step out and work toward your goals. They would like you to stay at their level because it gives off the illusion that nothing can be done to change their circumstances. When you make the impossible possible, it shows them the harsh reality that says anything can be done. They get that they are the only person holding them back. So, don't let people make you feel guilty because you want to progress. Don't settle for average when you have talents to give to the world.

Sometimes, people put the blame they should take responsibility for on you. It's a reflection of self-hatred. They may have made bad choices or didn't put in the effort you did, causing them to miss opportunities that you took. They get upset at you because they don't want to be upset with themselves. They want you to hate yourself for who you are because they aren't comfortable with the person they are. In that case, they need to really learn to love themselves versus trying to hurt more people.

You can't possibly let someone else tell you how you feel about yourself. You have the power to determine who you are. Other people either need to accept that or move on.

I must mention that not all of this is done intentionally. Usually, those who hurt you don't set out on a mission to do so. Often, they don't even realize they are hurting you. Even if they are aware, it may be hard for them to determine how to resolve those issues given their character or personal struggles. Unfortunately, some people will never change, so the hurt will continue if you allow it.

I believe forgiveness becomes easier when you move from being angry with that person to feeling sorry for them. Once I started to feel sympathy toward those who hurt me, I realized the issue wasn't with me. There were deeper issues at work that I couldn't fix. I was just the person who happened to be affected by those unresolved issues.

Here's my secret: don't take everything personally. The hurt may have been done *to* you, but it isn't *about* you. For every person who hurt me, I can probably name plenty of people they treated in a similar manner. You must accept that there are just some people who can't show compassion. There are others who can't seem to take responsibility for their actions, and you will never get an apology out of them. Sadly, there are just some people who refuse to believe they have done anything wrong, and you are probably not going to be the person to make them realize the error in their ways.

If someone has been disrespectful since 1982, what makes you think that you will force them to change?

Even if people are hurting themselves or totally oblivious to the consequences of their actions, that doesn't change the fact that they are toxic to you. If they are hurting you physically, emotionally, mentally, or financially, then that classifies them as being damaging or toxic. The definition doesn't change, regardless of relationship status, age, personality traits, etc. Toxic people are still harmful to our wellbeing no matter how we try to justify it.

Too many people excuse the actions of others by saying, "That's just the way he is" or "She's always been that way." They say this as if they have to put up with it because it's somehow part of that person's nature. Even if that is how he or she behaves, you have the choice whether to tolerate that behavior.

Of course, toxic people will make you feel guilty for being upset, or act as if you are being unreasonable when you choose not to put up with that behavior. However, holding on to those people by refusing to forgive is going to do more damage to you than them. Like holding on to a hot plate, you have to let go at some point to avoid being burned. Meanwhile, they are just standing by, watching you hold on to that pain.

For your own good, let it go. Do it for yourself.

I think many of us miss the point of forgiveness because we think we are doing it for the other person. Often, we don't realize that we forgive for our own sake, so we aren't driving ourselves crazy thinking of what was done and why. It releases us of the heaviness that comes with holding on to the hurt. It gives us permission to move past that hurt. It has nothing to do with the state of your relationship with that person, or the future of that relationship.

We refuse to forgive (or think someone has not forgiven us) because we get forgiveness and reconciliation confused. We think it is one in the same, but it's not. Keep in mind that forgiveness does not mean you need to have a relationship or even stay in contact with that person.

Simply put, restoration of a relationship does not have to come with the act of forgiveness.

It would be nice, but life doesn't often work that way.

We must understand that forgiveness does not guarantee a happy reunion. The sooner we learn that lesson, the easier it is to move on.

Forgiveness simply means that you aren't going to let that person's toxic behavior continue to inflict pain in your life. That's it. Whether you continue to have contact with that person after forgiveness is extended is completely up to you.

Too many people feel guilty because they forgave but cut off all communication. There is no need to feel condemned. Remember that you have the right to forgive and then move on for your overall wellbeing. I'm sure Jesus forgave Judas for betraying him, but nowhere does it imply that Judas would have remained in his circle. If Jesus knew it was sometimes best to forgive and let go, then why can't you do the same?

On the other hand, I also hear people say someone hasn't really forgiven them because they decided it was best that they not build a close relationship with them. They will say someone isn't forgiving because they decided not to pick up where they left off. The point of it all is that they don't have to—you can forgive and move on with the relationship or you can forgive and let it go. This isn't based on refusing to forgive, but that you must do what is best for you.

As a child, you learned not to touch the stove when it's hot. You came to the conclusion that every time you touched the stove you ended up getting hurt. Just because you develop a better understanding of how a stove works doesn't mean you are going to keep touching it. If anything, it makes you more aware of how dangerous it is to play around a hot stove. You learn your lesson and protect yourself, even if that means moving away from it. So, don't continuously go back to a situation where the person is unwilling or unable to change. You must let toxic people stay at a distance or remove yourself from them altogether.

As my mom would say, "How many times are you going to get kicked in the behind before you realize it hurts?"

Chapter Seven:

No More Negative Thinking

> "Happiness is a state of being. It's something you work for in the moment."

You already know that negative thinking about yourself hurts your self-esteem. However, negative thinking about your situation hurts your ability to experience true joy. Since happiness is something you work for in the moment, the ability to be content requires staying in the moment. This is called mindfulness. You are mindful of the here and now without thinking about the past or the future. Instead, you focus on the gift of the present. However, we have many thought patterns that decrease our mindfulness. These thoughts include playing the "If" game, thinking in extremes, entertaining worries, and having flat thoughts instead of 4D thinking. All leave us frustrated and defeated.

In this chapter, we will discuss those negative thought patterns and how you can beat them by practicing mindfulness. This is particularly helpful for those in mental distress as depression and anxiety come from an excess of negative thoughts. If you can stop those thoughts in their tracks, you have a better handle on your mental and emotional state.

IF-THEN THINKING

"We make a habit of putting our happiness on hold because we're waiting for something to occur in order to access it. This guarantees that you will be unhappy indefinitely."

~~~~~~~~

The "If" game is played when you decide what needs to happen in order to determine when you will be happy. As we know from uncovering unrealistic expectations, it's what I call the "ransom note syndrome." We give life our list of demands and then determine how we feel based upon what we get back. We need to be honest with ourselves and start approaching life as if it owes us nothing, because that's exactly how life is set up. Life isn't supposed to provide you with anything. So, you see, everything you have, big or small, is an unexpected blessing. Life doesn't owe you a family, a house, a job, a car … nothing. So, stop trying to wait until those things happen to enjoy your day.

We make a habit of putting our happiness on hold because we're waiting for something to occur in order to access it. This guarantees that you will be unhappy indefinitely because, one, more than likely, what we are waiting for won't make us as happy as we would like to believe it will, and, two, once we get it, something else will take its place.

For instance, let's say I'm upset because I don't have a car. I mope around stating that if I had a car then I would be happier because I would be able to get to more places, etc.

I spend about two years being bitter until I have the money to buy a car. I'm excited about finally having a car, until a few weeks pass by and I realize I wasn't missing as much as I thought. The places I really needed to get to were within walking distance, and it wasn't all that bad taking the bus to the mall.

In fact, it was more interesting seeing who came on the bus instead of enduring the stress of driving. Now, I'm still upset. However, I don't know why I'm upset because the car was supposed to solve that. So, I have to search my inventory to figure out something else I don't have that will fix the sorrow. In searching, I find out it's not really the car that was going to make me happy ... it was the fact that I don't own a house. Yes, that's it. I have a car, but I hate being at home because my apartment is too small. If I could have enough space to invite company over then I would be just fine. As a result, I put my hope in finally being content with a new home instead. I spend the next five years angry that I live in a tiny apartment thinking that if that changes, then I will really be happy, and the cycle continues.

Let me be totally honest with you. There is no winning here. As long as you search, you will find things you don't have that you think are the missing pieces to happiness. In reality, the only thing that's missing is your ability to see the situation clearly. There is no waiting to be happy. You must understand that you have the power to be happy regardless of what you think you want at the time.

EXTREME THINKING

"Having an all-or-nothing mentality will cause you to always be upset or sets you up so that nothing makes you happy."

~~~~~~~~

Thinking in terms of black and white will stop you from enjoying life. That's because most things in life happen in the gray area between the two extremes. This means that having an all-or-nothing mentality will cause you to always be upset or will set you up so nothing makes you happy.

Either your day was great or it was really bad. It can never be a good day with a few mishaps. Depending on how you feel, you either have the greatest job ever or you hate going to work. It's never just a stressful day at a job that you otherwise enjoy. You will either have enough money or focus on being broke. It's not that you had enough money to pay your bills, but just couldn't afford your $100 suit at the time.

Since life falls somewhere in the middle, you will constantly fall short of having a perfect day. Without a perfect day, you can't have joy. Perfect days don't exist, so your joy is put on hold indefinitely. Instead, think of your day as if you were doing a pros and cons list. If the pros outweigh the cons, you just had a good day. So that way, if you spilled soda on your keyboard at work, it's listed as a con. It's not the determining factor for whether you had a miserable day.

EXCESSIVE WORRYING

"We like to sit there during a time where we could have peace of mind to worry about a situation that might disturb our peace of mind."

~~~~~~~

I decided to perform an experiment. I told myself that the next worrisome situation that presented itself would be handled differently. I wouldn't fret over all the possible outcomes. I wouldn't dwell on the worst-case scenario. I would not let it ruin the time I spent waiting for the outcome. I actually forgot about the problem until that Monday because I didn't want to ruin my holiday weekend.

The whole point of my experiment was to see if worrying changed the outcome.

I found out that it didn't change the outcome, but it did change my outlook.

It changed my ability to experience joy and peace.

Growing up, many of us get the idea that worrying about a problem will solve it. That's because many problems can be solved if we think of the right solutions. However, if the situation is out of our control, sitting there dwelling on possible solutions is a complete waste of time. Yet we do it anyway. We figure it gives us something to do while we wait. It also tricks us into thinking we are doing our part in solving the problem. We think the energy we put into worrying somehow means we tried our best to generate a favorable outcome. However, that's not problem solving. That's torture.

We like to sit there during a time where we could have peace of mind to worry about a situation that might disturb our peace of mind.

Now, you just made it twice as hard to deal with the situation. You miss the time where you could have peace, and find yourself completely exhausted when it's time to face the facts. Therefore, I reminded myself that regardless of how much I stressed myself out, the results would be the same on Monday morning. So, I might as well have a good time while I wait.

The old Nicole would have dwelled on the problem all weekend. It would have ruined her holiday. She would have been stressed out and exhausted by Monday morning. Then she would have been upset with herself for ruining her weekend when the problem wasn't that bad at all.

This time that didn't happen.

First, I was able to enjoy my weekend by focusing on the present. Second, I wasn't fatigued from a worrisome weekend. Next, I decided to run errands instead of taking my usual nap due to mental exhaustion. Finally, I wasn't mad at myself for ruining the holiday. I was glad I didn't waste days on end being upset just to receive the same results.

In the end, the problem wasn't that bad after all.

While the outcome stayed the same, I changed. I made things different by dealing with what I could control—my peace of mind. Now, I'm trying to stop other people from worrying so they can experience the same peace.

FLAT THOUGHTS VERSUS FOUR-DIMENSIONAL THINKING

"Of course, everything looks good on the surface. It's when you really start examining beneath the surface that you start to second-guess many of your assumptions about happiness."

~~~~~~~

If you draw a cube on a piece of paper, all you will see is a square on a flat surface. This would be seeing the cube in 2D or the second dimension. It's what I like to call flat thinking. We see what's on the surface. We know nothing else about the cube. We don't see all sides of the cube and we can't really determine its actual size.

Thinking in 3D or the third dimension allows us to see that square as we would in real life. One that has four sides, a top, a bottom, etc. Most of us fall into this level of thinking. This means we can look at a situation from multiple angles. We know there is more than what meets the eye. Yet most of us stay stuck at this level. We see everything from the outside looking in.

Thinking in 4D or the fourth dimension means you see the cube in 3D, but you would also see what it looks like from inside the cube. It's no longer just an object, but an experience. When examining a situation, very few of us choose to think at this level. We don't necessarily put ourselves inside that scenario. We are aware that there is more to the story, but we hardly put ourselves in the shoes of others. We don't visualize ourselves in that exact situation to determine the best steps to take.

The best way to describe this would be to imagine a house. Flat thoughts (2D thinking) would be like looking at the blueprint or sketch of that house. We don't know what it looks like aside from the flat picture of a house. We definitely can't walk around and view the backyard. We can't go inside. We just look at a picture. In 3D, you see the house from all sides. You see walls, all sides of the roof, and so forth. You can even take a look at the backyard. Four-dimensional or 4D thinking means you can walk into that house and see what it looks like inside. When you get to that point, you truly get to know the house.

You see, thinking in such a way helps with the comparisons we make that zap our joy. When we see a wedding picture, we automatically think those people are happy. We see a two-dimensional picture that indicates happiness. Many of us thinking in 3D will see a few different sides if we know the people in the photo. We'll know they had their share of arguments and other marital problems.

Thinking in 4D causes you to ask the questions: Given what I know, how would I feel being in that situation? If I were married to person X, would I be happy? What would I think of my experience? How long would that feeling last?

I say this not to be discouraging, but to get you to see the situation for what it is given all the facts. I'm also not saying that your pain isn't valid or that one person's pain is more real than the next. I'm saying that everything looks good until you really examine the matter. As long as you are looking at smiling pictures, a photo of a "sold" sign, or a giggling baby, you are going to start comparing your life based off two-dimensional facts.

Of course, everything looks good on the surface. It's when you really start examining beneath the surface that you second-guess many of your assumptions about happiness. That is because 4D thinking will let you know that possibly living with someone for the rest of your life can be a tough task whether you love the person or not. Four-dimensional thinking allows you to see that "sold" sign and remember all the thousands of dollars that went into the house. It will remind you of all the nights the family went hungry to save up for that house while you were out at that new restaurant with your friends. That baby (as cute as it may be) may not just represent joy, but also frustration over figuring out how to be a good parent. It may represent anxiety as you hope for a healthy child.

This isn't just acknowledging that there is more to a situation than what you see. It's actually forcing you to place yourself in that scenario. Chances are if you aren't jumping for joy once you start reevaluating, then that thing or event you desperately want will not be the source of all joy. Of course, it's nice to have a partner, a huge home, or a newborn. However, we quickly stop ourselves from saying "Why me?" when we realize the amount of work and responsibility that goes into having those things in our lives. It stops us from thinking negatively about why we don't have those things when we consider that while those things will bring us some form of joy, it still won't make us happy all the time. There are other factors at play.

Many of us think in such a negative, envious way because we are in love with the notion of joy. However, we aren't seeing enough of the situation to really get that envy under control. It's like being famous. Most people like the idea of being famous but wouldn't be happy when faced with the pressure. Flat or 2D thinking says, "I wish I were famous. I want all those people admiring me." Four-dimensional (4D) thinking says, "It would be nice to be famous, but I find more joy in actually being able to go out to dinner without a crowd of people holding cameras over my table."

Now it's less appealing.

So the key to dealing with negative thinking, like criticism and unhealthy comparisons, is to think of all the factors you don't want to see. Look beyond the appealing factors to those that aren't so attractive.

I believe there is a reason for everything. It's just very hard to see that when you are going through the situation. With a 4D mindset, I look at the facts a bit differently. Yes, that job was given to someone else, but then I see the person who landed a similar job complaining that the stress of the workplace is making her sick. Then I'm thankful I didn't get the job. I simply know that I will find a job that fits me (rather than envying someone else while looking in from the outside).

I tell people going through difficult times with employment or finances that what is for them will be. You don't have to be religious to believe in destiny. If you didn't get that job, it's because you weren't supposed to have that job. Whatever job is for you will find its way to you. I know that's hard to understand when you are unemployed and broke. However, trust me, your sanity is worth more than your salary.

It's not what you have that makes you happy; it's what you do with what you have that counts. If you are too busy looking at everyone else, you become less content with yourself. Then you will fail to realize that joy is not in the possessions you hold, but in how you hold those possessions. If you find the joy in what you are given, then you are more likely to be content rather than looking for more stuff to measure your happiness.

THE NEED TO PRACTICE MINDFULNESS

"We ruin the moment we are in by using it to think about other moments in the past or those yet to come. Essentially, we let our past into our present. We let the future steal the show before it even arrives."

~~~~~~~~

Mindfulness is simply about focusing on the present. Negativity and worrying comes in when we are focused more on the past or the future. In either case, we are wasting the gift of the present moment. When you are in the moment, you are only focusing on getting the best out of what's taking place now. It's hard to truly enjoy yourself in the now and worry about everything that needs to happen later. That's essentially what worry and negative thinking does to us. It takes us away from truly enjoying the present moment. We are so caught up that we ignore the present by dwelling on the past or the future.

We ruin the present moment by thinking about other moments in the past or those yet to come. Essentially, we let our past into our present. We let the future steal the show before it even arrives. The Dalai Lama once revealed, "There are only two days in the year that nothing can be done. One is called yesterday and the other is called tomorrow, so today is the right day to love, believe, do and mostly live."

Mindfulness takes practice. You will find that you will

have to monitor your thoughts and force them out the way. You will have to keep reminding yourself to just focus on what's going on around you at the time. It's difficult because we are so used to having multiple things on our mind. However, we need to start thinking differently for our overall mental health. It is worth the effort.

You can start with little things, like focusing on the movie you are watching without thinking about where you are going out to eat afterwards. Then slowly build your way up to avoiding thoughts about other future events, like what work you have to complete tomorrow. You force your mind to enjoy what's present so you don't miss the joy of what's taking place right before your eyes, not letting that chance to experience true happiness pass you by. The present is a gift, and we need to start seeing the beauty in that treasure.

Chapter Eight:
Eat Smart, Plan Well

> *"If you want to get this 'happiness' thing right, you need to treat your body right as well. Your physical health is tied to your mental health in more ways than you can imagine."*

My grandfather became a vegetarian long before I was born (in spite of the rumor that he made the best BBQ). He also made the decision to quit smoking. He's one of the few people I've known that can make a choice and actually stick with it once and for all. He just decided he didn't want to eat meat anymore, so he stopped. He quit smoking cold turkey.

I tried being a vegetarian multiple times. Usually, Sunday dinner or holidays ruined my efforts. When my grandfather would ask what happened, I would tell him that every time I tried to become a vegetarian I was presented with meat. He would say, "Just because it's in front of you doesn't mean you have to eat it."

I admired my grandfather for taking care of his health. Even in spite of all his efforts, he would jokingly state, "If I knew I would live this long, I would have taken better care of myself."

My grandfather passed away a few months before his 80th birthday, but he lived a full, healthy life. He ran more miles for exercise in his 60s than I could at half that age. His mind was sharp. He learned how to use the computer around the time I went off to college. He then bought one of his own. Somehow, he set up instant messenger with his own screen name. It's kind of weird getting a message or an email from your grandfather as a college student.

However, it was commendable because he never let his age determine his happiness. He found what made him happy even as a senior citizen. He also understood how your physical health determined your mental health. I guess that's why they called him the "man with the million dollar smile."

Seriously, I rarely saw him without a smile.

Because of him, I started looking more into what good health actually meant and if it could change your emotions. I admit that I'm still trying to practice these health tips, but I am now aware that many foods and vitamins can help with good mental health. I am also aware that certain foods should be avoided, especially if you struggle with stress or other forms of mental distress like depression, anxiety, manic depression, or panic disorder. If you want to get this "happiness" thing right, you need to treat your body right as well. Your physical health is tied to your mental health in more ways than you can imagine.

Here are just some of the lessons I learned:

- Low levels of various vitamins such as Vitamin D affect mental health.

- Certain foods can help boost your mood, while others can trigger anxiety.

- High levels of sugar, sodium, and caffeine cause mental instability.

- Exercise not only lowers stress hormones but also boosts mood hormones.

- Lack of sleep causes more problems than grumpiness.

In this chapter, I will cover vitamins and supplements that help with brain function, as well as foods and beverages to consume to boost your mood. I will also discuss what to avoid or limit to alleviate symptoms of depression or anxiety (stress), or to regulate mood swings. We will discuss the steps you can take for your diet to achieve better mental health. Please discuss taking any of these steps with your medical doctor and receive approval before starting any diet or exercise program.

First, for good mental health you need to remember the five chemicals that influence brain function. When these chemicals are off, then you are off. Your brain chemistry must be stable and produced in the right amount in order to maintain good health. The chemicals for optimal brain function are:

Chemical	Function
Dopamine	Tells body to move or react
Endorphins	Boosts mood and reduces pain
Oxytocin	Good feeling produced when shown affection (the feeling you get when you cuddle or receive a hug)
Norepinephrines	Gives body energy to fight stress
Serotonin	Maintains mood function

Sources: medicalnewstoday.com, psychologytoday.com,.about.com

Vitamins, supplements, and antioxidants are essential to body and brain function. In fact, many of the chemicals needed for optimal brain function can be found in various foods.

Vitamins/Supplements	Function	Examples
Antioxidants	Repairs damaged cells Fights cancer Lowers depression	Apples Berries Onions Garlic Dark Chocolate Avocado
B Vitamins (Folic Acid)	Boosts mood and energy	Leafy green vegetables Fruits Fortified grains Beans Avocado Asparagus

Vitamins/Supplements	Function	Examples
Vitamin C	Boost immune system Lowers stress	Oranges Berries
Vitamin D	Boosts mood	Indoor/Outdoor light Milk Salmon
Vitamin E	Fights depression	Avocado Leafy green vegetables
Fiber	Pushes toxins and stress hormones out the body	Oatmeal Lentils (beans) Apples
Magnesium	Helps mood function	Nuts Seeds
Omega 3 Fatty Acids/ Alpha-Linoleic Acid	Helps overall brain function	Walnuts Apples Tomatoes Fish Oil/ Cod Liver Oil
Probiotics	Healthy bacteria for the intestines (90% of Serotonin produced)	Supplement

Vitamins/Supplements	Function	Examples
SAM- E	Helps in the transmission of mood hormones	Supplement
St. John Wort	Acts as natural antidepressant	Supplement **Takes 4-6 weeks to get full effect.

Sources: about.com, everydayhealth.com, medicalnewstoday.com

You might also need to eliminate or limit foods to reduce symptoms of depression and anxiety (stress). Many of the vitamins found in the foods previously mentioned help to fight stress (antioxidants, B-Vitamins, Vitamin C). However, some foods and beverages can create the opposite effect when consumed, such as sugary foods and alcohol.

Please note that while tea is listed as one of the caffeinated beverages to avoid, herbal tea may prove beneficial. Chamomile tea promotes sleep and lowers stress. Green tea gives brain power. Despite being caffeinated, Green tea also has anti-cancer properties. The best advice is to consult your doctor and take everything in moderation.

Foods & Beverages	Effect	Examples
Alcohol	Temporarily relaxes your body before creating mood swings	Any alcoholic beverage
Caffeine	Temporarily boasts mood and worsens mood swings when depleted	Black Tea Coffee Soda
Sodium	Impacts blood pressure and causes heart problems	Salty foods Soda
Sugar	Worsens mood swings when depleted	Sweets Soda Sweetened juices

Sources: about.com, everydayhealth.com, prevention.com, livestrong.com

Chapter Nine:

Self-Care Is a Must

"Self-care is not optional; it is a survival tool."

Stress not only wreaks havoc on your body but your mind as well. Stress can significantly lower your immune system, which can cause mental health issues such as eating disorders, depression, mania, and anxiety. That's because stress causes the body and brain to work overtime.

Cortisol, or the stress hormone, helps in small amounts. It gives us a quick boost in mood and increases our ability to tolerate pain. However, large amounts of this stress hormone in your bloodstream can have the opposite effect. It can lower your immune system response and lead to cognitive impairment. Think of it like sugar levels. We need a certain amount of sugar in our bloodstream for energy, but a large amount of it leads to diabetes. Therefore, the large amount of cortisol that is produced when you are stressed leads to various health issues.

These stress hormones throw our bodies off track to the point where it is hard to function properly. This is why we shouldn't make major decisions when under pressure. It's also part of the reason why we can't seem to manage activities too well when we are stressed out. The same normal functions we would perform every day become twice as hard to handle. It is also the reason why we should consider exercising for mental health reasons as well as physical ones. You may have been told that exercise helps release endorphins to make you happy. However, it also lowers your cortisol levels so you can literally get rid of the stress in your body.

Unfortunately, we ignore that stress and attempt to function under pressure. That is why taking care of your body is a must if you want to maintain good mental health or be of help to others. Most of us claim we don't have the time or the need to take care of ourselves. We think everyone else can take a break but ourselves.

Let's be clear.

Self-care is not optional; it is a survival tool.

Self-care is doing what your mind and body needs to unwind, recharge, or relax. It can be exercise, meditation, listening to music, taking in the scenery outside, or taking a bubble bath. It is whatever helps you to get back to a place of strength and peace. This also includes getting the recommended 8 to 9 hours of sleep each night. Your body repairs and rejuvenates itself during this time. So you cut your body's ability to restore if you decide to miss out on those critical hours of sleep. (I admit I'm still working on my sleeping habits.)

I've noticed that most people who have poor mental health are also people pleasers, perfectionists, and extreme nurturers who consume themselves with the concerns of others or are generally too helpful. Basically, they care too much. In fact, they care about other people's problems more than the person with the problem. As a result, they put their mental health on the backburner. They take care of everyone but themselves. Sometimes it just comes out of a genuine need to go above and beyond for others. At other times, it's a matter of self-esteem. This is why I said self-esteem plays a heavy role in mental health. If I don't feel I deserve to get rest over the constant demand of others, I'm going to burn out. That stress can ultimately lead to depression and anxiety as I try to run on fumes.

Therefore, while it seems like a noble act to put the needs of others before your own, it's actually quite unhealthy. If you aren't getting what you need, then you can't possibly be in the best shape to help others. You can only give what you have in terms of attention and energy. If you don't have any energy to spend, then everyone suffers. You exhaust yourself, and the people you want to help end up getting what's left over. So, you are taking care of others when you take care of yourself.

The first step to self-care is coming up with a plan that is unique to your needs. What calms one person may not be the best for someone else. You have to take inventory of all the things you would like to do. You would then need to carve time in your schedule to do those things that will help you get back on track. When choosing self-care activities, try not to pick something work-related. Also, try not to use social media as a self-care technique because, as we learned previously, it can cause stress on some levels.

Self-Care Examples:

- Talking a walk, going to the park, or sitting outside to enjoy nature

- Prayer/meditation

- Music therapy (you may lack energy, but you can press the play button)

- Light therapy (good for those who live in colder climates)

- Taking a nap (look into sleep apps or techniques if you have insomnia)

- Taking a bubble bath

- Reading your favorite book or magazine

- Watching your favorite show/movie

- Finding a comedy special to watch to increase laughter

- Going window shopping (that way you aren't spending money)

- Writing in your journal

- Reading the Bible or other scriptures (positive messages help as well)

- Finding a hobby with arts & crafts such as painting, crocheting, etc.

- Buying crayons and a coloring book (it's not just for kids anymore)

- Gardening

- Calling up a friend for a chat or to plan a night out

- Taking a mini-vacation (even if it's a trip close by for the weekend)

- Going to church or other religious service

- Practicing mindfulness through meditation, yoga, or deep breathing

- Exercise (or just stretching if you are too tired to do a routine)

- Dancing around the house (which counts as exercise)

- Watching funny video clips

- Starting a book club or support group with your friends (bring good snacks)

- Planning an upcoming event (Super Bowl party, birthday celebration)

- Trying your new favorite restaurant

- Hosting a movie night with friends

Chapter Ten:

Secure a Safety Plan

> *"If you never see a pattern, your emotional state will appear chaotic at best."*

Much of managing your mental health is being proactive instead of reactive. You can't wait until you are already in a depressive state or anxious about any and everything to take measures. You should already have a plan in place that will help you when you notice your mood is off. That means the minute you feel as if you are getting depressed or worrying a bit too much, you have a plan in place to make sure you get back on track.

Most mental health professionals call this a safety plan.

A safety plan is based on steps that you can stick with when you find yourself feeling bad or unsafe. I would suggest that if you are seriously considering suicide that you call 911 or go to the emergency room for help. You may also consider contacting a suicide hotline to talk with someone for as long as you need to do so.

Unfortunately, going to the hospital for mental health issues can often become just as scary as your feelings at the moment. Therefore, many people refuse to go. It's not necessarily the fear of going to the hospital, but what you experience once you are there. Many facilities are poorly funded or understaffed. While many places do their best to separate patients by their needs, it is likely that you will be placed with those suffering from more severe mental issues that deal with psychosis. I understand that this can be scary for someone who may be dealing with a common bout of depression or anxiety.

Let's be real. Most people aren't thinking of going to the hospital as their first resort, so having a plan in place to prevent that is best. However, if you need to go to the hospital, my advice would be to remain calm, befriend nurses and staff members who are sensitive to your concerns, and have someone you can call for support. As an alternative, try to spend the night at a loved one's house. Having someone watch you to make sure you are safe is the main idea.

Your safety plan should include at least two emergency contacts and a hotline number. This doesn't have to be a suicide hotline, but any service number you can call to speak to someone when feeling down. They are there to listen. It might be helpful to place those emergency contacts in your phone under "favorites" or put them on speed dial. It takes the guesswork out of getting in touch with someone when you are already feeling overwhelmed.

You also want to list critical information that you need to track. This will help others if they need to know of your condition. For instance, if you need to go to the hospital, they will already have the information needed to treat you. This information should include any medications or vitamins you are taking at the time. Make sure you list the name of the medication or vitamin, the dosage, and how many times a day you take them. Make sure you also list any allergies. This may seem obvious when you are in a good mood, but it needs to be noted when you are feeling out of sorts or some-one needs to monitor you.

As part of your safety plan, you also need to note various situations that affect your mood. For each situation, list some signals that your mood is declining and the trigger or trig-gers that cause you to feel that way. Write down anything that starts the process of those feelings. This will also help to re-mind you of what to manage on a daily basis. Write down as much as you can think of: job stress, anniversaries, missing medication, not taking a break for at least an hour, violent or emotional shows, sad stories, not eating breakfast, etc.

For example, one of the signals you are getting depressed is withdrawing from others. A trigger may be experiencing stress on the job.

For each trigger, you will need a healthy plan or activity to release those emotions. So, if you know watching violent movies makes you angry, then you may want to list what you will do when those feelings come creeping up. Are you going to put on calming music? Are you going to play video games to get your mind off of it? Are you going to follow up by watching a comedy to clear your mind? You have to decide what will work based on the emotions you feel at the time. As a suggestion, I would write down the movies and music that help. Make a collection of movies for the occasion or a music playlist with songs that help you feel better. The only restriction to creating your plan is that you make sure that your release is healthy and constructive. Going out for drinks might not be the best way to control your anger or anxiety.

I've provided my version of a safety plan based off the template created by Barbara Stanley and Gregory K. Brown. More information about safety plans can be found on the National Suicide Prevention Line website at www.suicidepreventionlifeline.org. I hope that it will prove beneficial to you. I've redesigned it to include additional information I feel is most important when in distress. You can add or modify as you see fit. You can also update your safety plan as your mood and circumstances change. That is okay and expected.

EXAMPLE SAFETY PLAN

Emergency Contacts	Friend A 555-5555	Neighbor 888-1111	Suicide Hotline 1-800-273-TALK	Emergency Room 911
Medications/ Vitamins	Multivitamin	Blood Pressure Med "A"	Antidepressant Med "B"	Mood Stabilizer Med "C"
Dose	n/a	20 mg	50 mg	10 mg
Times Per Day	1	1	2	1
Allergies	Peanuts	Pollen		

Situation A	Signals (s)	Triggers(s)	Action Plan
	Withdrawing from others	Job stress	Take 30 minute break
			Text Friend A
			Pray/Meditate
Situation B	Sadness Hopelessness	Sad News Stories	Watch a funny movie
			Call Friend A

It may be difficult to find your triggers and what action plan to take if you are not aware of how you react to situations or see patterns to your behavior. If you never see a pattern, your emotional state will appear chaotic at best. That's why I recommend keeping a tracking journal or calendar. Try to find your mood pattern over the course of the day, week, or month. I've provided a sample tracking calendar based off how I track my mood. I hope it will help you as well.

A tracking calendar should take you through your day so you are able to pinpoint what activities impact your mood the most. At the start of each day, try to rate your mood from 1-10 (1 being extremely low to 10 being extremely high). Write down how many hours of sleep you had the night before out of the recommended eight to nine hours. Next, write down what you ate for breakfast, lunch, and dinner. Be sure to note the time you had your meals and mention any snacks you consumed.

You will want to write a list of things you did for the day. Try to add the amount of time spent doing each activity. For example, you can jot down that you went to work for eight hours and then volunteered at the local soup kitchen for an hour afterwards. Then list what you did in terms of free time or self-care for the day. See chapter 9 on self-care for a list of activities you can try to relax. Finally, describe how you feel overall and rate your mood (1-10) before bedtime.

From viewing the example tracking calendar, you can see many patterns forming from Monday to Wednesday. You will see that:

- Skipping lunch was probably not a good idea

- Nine hours of sleep on Tuesday night resulted in a mood increase on Wednesday

- Watching comedy seems to work to boost mood

- Listening to music in the evening helps with sleep

EXAMPLE TRACKING CALENDAR

Date:	Monday July 20, 2015	Tuesday July 21, 2015	Wednesday July 22, 2015
Day Mood: (1-10)	7	5	9
Hours of Sleep (0-9)	5	7	9
Breakfast: 7 PM	Apple Juice Cereal bar	Oatmeal Orange Juice	Fiber rich cereal Orange juice
Lunch: 12 PM	Skipped Lunch	Chicken Salad	Kale Salad with Turkey Sandwich
Dinner: 7 PM	Potatoes, Steak, Greens	Beef Soup	Chicken, Rice, Green Beans
Snack(s):	Apple (1:00 p.m.) Strawberries (1:00 a.m.)	Orange (1:00 p.m.) Almonds (8:00 p.m.)	Yogurt (5:00 p.m.)
Glasses of Water (0-8)	3	7	5
Day Activities	Work - 8 hours Volunteer - 2 hours	Work - 8 hours Laundry - 2 hours	Work - 8 hours Errands - 3 hours
Self-Care Measures	Listened to Music -1 hour	Watched Comedy Special - 1 hour	Went to restaurant with friend - 1 hour Listened to Music -1 hour

Date:	Monday July 20, 2015	Tuesday July 21, 2015	Wednesday July 22, 2015
Description of Day/Night	Job was really stressful. Hard to fall asleep last night thinking of the work week. Going to bed early.	Went to bed earlier last night and decided to drink more water. Watching my comedy special helped.	Tired from running errands. Able to concentrate on most of my tasks. Music helped me unwind.
Night Mood: (1-10)	5	8	9

Once again, these observations may seem like common sense. However, sometimes it's hard to find obvious patterns if you aren't paying attention. As you can see, writing down your thoughts for three days will give you enough to consider. In just a few days, you will learn some of your triggers, what works in terms of self-care, how meal patterns impact your mood, and how much sleep you need to function. All of this information gives you something to work with when considering your self-care activities and safety plan. Documenting your mood helps you to monitor what's occurring instead of taking a guess at how your week is going. When you are certain of what's taking place, you can begin to take healthy measures to live your best.

Conclusion

> *"We must carry our mental health as a prized possession, taking the time to care for it as our very lives depend on it."*

The journey to joy is never an easy one. However, we can all agree that it is well worth it. Our mental health is something that we should cherish. Unfortunately, many of us don't hold it in high regard. We treat our physical ailments, but we shove our mental ones under the rug. Instead of proudly embarking on our journey to joy, we would rather climb the mountain of misery.

It's time we start taking better care of ourselves. It's time we start caring about the mental health of our loved ones.

We will no longer allow the stigma of addressing mental health to stand in the way of our very wellbeing. We will not allow society to cause us to suffer in silence. We can no longer stand by watching others struggle without the support they need. We must carry our mental health as a prized possession—taking the time to care for it as our very lives depend on it.

I hope that you've enjoyed this journey, and that the tips in this book help you as you travel along. I certainly hope it has given you the power to claim the happiness that you so deserve.

Know that you are unstoppable and that you are loved. If no one seems to understand, trust that I care.

Never give up.

Your best is yet to come, and you will see the best when you stay the course.

Love,

Nicole

Helpful Resources for the Journey

American Foundation for Suicide Prevention

> http://www.afsp.org
>
> **National Suicide Prevention Lifeline**
>
> 1-800-273-TALK (8255)

American Psychological Association

> www.apa.org

Find a Psychologist:

> http://locator.apa.org/

National Alliance on Mental Illness (NAMI)

> www.nami.org

NAMI Helpline

> 800-950-6264

National Institute of Health (NIH)

www.nimh.gov

Substance Abuse and Mental Health Administration

www.samhsa.gov

References

Signs and Symptoms of Depression/Anxiety

National Alliance on Mental Illness. *Know the warning signs.* Retrieved November 25, 2015, from http://www.nami.org/Learn-More/Know-the-Warning-Signs.

Mood Hormones

Bergland, Christopher. (2012, Nov 29)." The neurochemicals of happiness: 7 brain molecules that make you feel great." *Psychology Today.* Retrieved November 25, 2015, from https://www.psychologytoday.com/blog/the-athletes-way/201211/the-neurochemicals-happiness.

McIntosh, James. (2015, June 26). "What is serotonin? What does serotonin do?" *Medical News Today.* Retrieved October 1, 2015, from, http://www.medicalnewstoday.com/articles/232248.php.

Purse, Marcia. *Norepinephrine*. (2015, February 14). Retrieved October 1, 2015, from, http://bipolar.about.com/od/glossary/g/gl_norepinephri.htm

Salters-Pedneault, Kristalyn, Ph.D. (2014, November 24). *Dopamine*. Retrieved October 1, 2015, from,

http://bpd.about.com/od/glossary/g/dopamine.htm.

Scott, Elizabeth. (2014, December 18). *Cortisol and stress: How to stay healthy*. Retrieved October 1, 2015, from, http://stress.about.com/od/stresshealth/a/cortisol.htm.

Vitamins/Supplements/Foods

Glassman, Keri. (2014, May 22). "13 foods that fight stress." *Prevention*. Retrieved October 1, 2015, from, http://www.prevention.com/mind-body/emotional-health/13-healthy-foods-reduce-stress-and-depression.

Iliades, Chris. (2012, April 18). "Foods that fight depression." *Everyday Health*. Retrieved October 1, 2015, from, http://www.everydayhealth.com/depression/foods-that-fight-depression.aspx.

McIntosh, James. (2015, September 17). "Adhering to a healthy diet could reduce risk of depression." *Medical News Today*. Retrieved October 1, 2015, from http://www.medicalnewstoday.com/articles/299490.php.

Wood-Moen, Robin. (2015, February 18). "Foods that trigger depression." *Livestrong.* Retrieved October 1, 2015, from, http://www.livestrong.com/article/351176-foods-that-trigger-depression/

Safety Plan

National Suicide Prevention Line. *How can a safety plan help?* Retrieved November 25, 2015, from http://www.suicidepreventionlifeline.org/learn/safety.aspx.

About the Author

DR. NICOLE M. ROBINSON is a mental health advisor who creates learning environments to help everyday people overcome depression and anxiety as a means of restoring and sustaining joy and fulfillment. Having personally triumphed mental distress  and dedicating her academic studies toward the experience, she is no stranger of being "sick and tired."

She earned a B.S. and an M.S. in Communication with an emphasis in Health Systems Administration from Rochester Institute of Technology. She later received her Ph.D. in Health Communication from George Mason University. Her research on the stigma of mental illness and cultural beliefs won the *Outstanding Research Project Award* at the 2013 DC Health Communication Conference, and she takes pride in being a member of the National Alliance on Mental Illness (NAMI).

Aside from saving lives through her gift of advocacy, she's also a poet who enjoys reading and spending time with her poodle, Missy.

To learn more, visit Dr. Robinson at www.unstoppable-joybook.com.

purposely
created
PUBLISHING

WE WANT TO HEAR FROM YOU!!!

If this book has made a difference in your life
Dr. Nicole would be delighted to hear about it.

Leave a review on Amazon.com!

BOOK DR. NICOLE TO SPEAK AT YOUR NEXT EVENT!

Send an email to: booking@publishyourgift.com

FOLLOW DR. NICOLE ON SOCIAL MEDIA

f /DrNicoleMRobinson   DoctorNicole1

"EMPOWERING YOU TO IMPACT GENERATIONS"
WWW.PUBLISHYOURGIFT.COM

CPSIA information can be obtained
at www.ICGtesting.com
Printed in the USA
FFOW01n1548300718
47520716-50912FF

9 781942 838760